ENERGY
RISING

JULIA DiGANGI

ENERGY RISING

The

NEUROSCIENCE

of LEADING *with*

EMOTIONAL POWER

HARVARD BUSINESS REVIEW PRESS
BOSTON, MASSACHUSETTS

The web addresses referenced in this book were live and correct at the time of the book's publication but may be subject to change.

Confidentiality/Medical Disclaimer: This book is not a substitute for personalized professional advice. The author is not rendering any form of mental health treatment. While this is a book about the concept of emotional pain, when suffering from a mental health condition, the reader should consult appropriate professionals before adopting practices in the book or making any inferences from it. All identifying details have been changed unless otherwise noted.

Library of Congress Cataloging-in-Publication Data

Names: DiGangi, Julia, author. | Harvard Business Review Press, issuing body.
Title: Energy rising : the neuroscience of leading with emotional power / Julia DiGangi.
Description: Boston, Massachusetts : Harvard Business Review Press, [2023] |
    Includes index.
Identifiers: LCCN 2023005643 (print) | LCCN 2023005644 (ebook) |
    ISBN 9781647823450 (hardcover) | ISBN 9781647825584 (epub)
Subjects: LCSH: Energy psychology. | Neuropsychology. | Control (Psychology) |
    Leadership.
Classification: LCC RC489.E53 D64 2023 (print) | LCC RC489.E53 (ebook) |
    DDC 616.89—dc23/eng/20230428
LC record available at https://lccn.loc.gov/2023005643
LC ebook record available at https://lccn.loc.gov/2023005644

ISBN: 978-1-64782-345-0
eISBN: 978-1-64782-558-4

The paper used in this publication meets the requirements of the American National Standard for Permanence of Paper for Publications and Documents in Libraries and Archives Z39.48-1992.

For all of us who, even when it hurts, keep rising

CONTENTS

Introduction

I want to have a conversation with you about your emotional power—your ability to stay strong in the midst of life's inevitable challenges. This book is dedicated to helping you transform your work, your relationships, and—most importantly—your own life by working more effectively with your emotional energy.

Your emotions are, in many ways, the final judge of your experiences. Are you successful enough? Depends. How do you *feel* about it? Is your life meaningful? Depends. How do you *feel* about it? Can you be more effective? Kinder? More confident? Are you a good manager, entrepreneur, parent, or partner? Depends.

How do you *feel* about it?

Until you understand how to work more effectively with your emotions, it's easy to expend tremendous energy yanking at ineffective levers of change. When we pull the wrong levers for too long, we feel stressed, frustrated, angry, and exhausted. Over time, we have the sense that our life is filled with too much resistance—that we're stuck in situations we don't like, jobs we don't want, and relationships we don't enjoy.

Your emotions are the bridge between where you currently stand and where you want to be. When you learn how to work with the energy of your emotions, you find empowerment, clarity, and satisfaction. Our conversation is dedicated to your emotional rising—to your ability to sustain your emotional strength even when your situations get tough.

To be clear, your emotional power is *not* the ability to eradicate all stress, fear, anxiety, disappointment, or other bad feelings from your life. Rather, your emotional power is your ability to rise even when your situations give you plenty of good reasons to stay down.

To do this, you must first understand what your emotions actually are: energy. I mean this physically. Your emotions are the product of a complex dance between electrical, chemical, and magnetic energies. Neuroscientists use several tools to track this brain-based choreography. Much of my work has used functional magnetic resonance imaging (fMRI) and electroencephalogram (EEG) technologies that let us see what happens in the brain when we provoke some type of emotion—fear, anger, happiness, and many others. With fMRI, we measure changes in the brain's chemical energy. EEG helps us measure spikes in the brain's electrical energy. Because these energy exchanges occur in predictable ways, neuroscientists can study the brain to create powerful, healing changes in people's lives.[1]

Your brain is, quite literally, the ultimate *electrical machine*. Sending electrical impulses traveling at speeds up to 260 miles an hour and catalyzing thousands of electrochemical reactions every second, your brain builds reality.[2] Look around. Everywhere you look you'll see evidence of human beings using brain energy to turn their emotions into thoughts and their thoughts into things. From technology to medicine to war to poetry, everything you can point to in the physical world had to first originate as a zap of electricity in the gelatinous three-pound blob inside someone's skull. If it were a science fiction movie, you wouldn't even believe it.

Have you ever tried to do something in your life—start a project, build a team, launch a business, begin a relationship, teach a child—that *should* have worked? In other words, you had the *right* strategy. You had the *right* people with the *right* plan who knew how to do the *right* things, but for some reason—a reason you can't quite articulate—it simply didn't work.

What you needed was the right energy. As you will see in the coming chapters, there isn't enough strategy in the world to fix bad energy, because your brain runs on energy, not on strategy. This book is based on a novel and simple premise: Your emotional power is best understood not as a set of activities you do or strategies you execute, **but as an energy you possess**. And when you learn to intelligently harness this energy, you begin to lead your life in the direction you desire.

Your brain's energy creates sensations that you then name various things—things like joy, anxiety, anger, stress, excitement, sorrow, love, hope, irritation, desire, and boredom. But when you really get down to it, all these emotions can really be distilled down to just two kinds of emotional energies: ones that hurt and ones that heal. For our conversation, we'll call these two energies:

- **Emotional pain:** any negative emotional sensation you feel. Although pain might sound like a catastrophic word—and sometimes it certainly can be—we'll use it broadly to represent *any type of negative sensation you feel.* You may commonly refer to these negative sensations as stress, anxiety, fear, anger, worry, frustration, irritation, embarrassment, shame, exhaustion, self-consciousness, inadequacy, disappointment, or jealousy.

- **Emotional power:** any emotional sensation that makes you feel you are worthy. You may commonly refer to these positive sensations as worthiness, confidence, strength, esteem, value, integrity, peace, resilience, significance, or importance.

In what I have come to understand as one of the greatest paradoxes of life, the depth of your emotional power relies directly on your ability to work with the energy of your emotional pain. When worked with wisely, it's the energy of emotional pain that, counterintuitively enough, strengthens you. If you've been stuck for long—feeling lost, confused, anxious, uninspired, *unempowered*—it's because you've been approaching pain the wrong way. To rise to new levels of your emotional power, you will have to accept one core counterintuitive premise: **that your emotional pain—all those negative feelings you keep trying to avoid—is often the precise path to your empowerment**.

A common response to painful negative feelings like stress, fear, worry, embarrassment, or anxiety is to try to avoid them. And so, we commonly avoid the conversations, people, places, and memories that cause us pain. The problem, however, is that chronic avoidance of your painful feelings doesn't end your feelings; it just exhausts you. All that ignoring, scrolling, pretending, numbing, and denying takes a tremendous amount of *actual* neuropsychological energy. Research shows that avoidance of our negative feelings wears us down.[3] The energy we spend persistently avoiding our painful feelings then creates more painful feelings in the form of exhaustion, burnout, depletion, and numbness.

The good news is there's solution. I'll offer you a set of practical strategies and tools I call the *neuroenergetics of emotional power*, a model I created through my work as a neuropsychologist. Neuroenergetics is simply the idea that our emotional lives run on the brain's real, physical energy. When we more clearly understand how the brain constructs our reality, we can engineer our lives in more satisfying and empowered ways. Neuroenergetics, rooted in neuroscience and psychology, will offer you access to new levels of your emotional power.

A bit about me: I'm a neuropsychologist. My work focuses on the connection between the brain, emotional pain, and emotional power. I've conducted various lines of research and examined brain function with colleagues in labs and clinics at Harvard, Columbia, Georgetown, the University of Chicago, DePaul, and the University of Illinois at Chicago. I've examined the brain, trauma, emotion, resilience, psychopathology, relationships, and genetics.[4] In addition to my research and clinical experience, I've worked with and learned from leaders at the highest levels of power, including the White House press office, global companies, international NGOs, and the military. Prior to becoming a neuropsychologist, I did international humanitarian aid and development, where I provided support in UN-declared emergency zones.

For many years, I've worked with individuals around the globe who have endured a range of emotional pain from extreme trauma to common stress. I've had the profound privilege of serving survivors of torture, genocide, sexual assault, domestic abuse, gun violence, and war. I also routinely serve managers, entrepreneurs, parents, couples, coworkers, and friends who endure the common yet heavy weight of what it means to be human. They struggle through anxieties about relationships, pressures about performance, fears about failures, worries about worth, and stresses about time. If you ever struggle with your feelings, I want to assure you: this book's for you.

While the causes and severity of our experiences can vary greatly, the underlying emotional energy and the solutions are strikingly similar. Pain is profoundly intimate and yet it bonds us in our universal humanity. Your pain, regardless of its form, can be used to power your transformation. I've watched many people—from professionals to parents to partners—come into a more intelligent relationship with their emotions. When they do, their lives, and the lives of the many people they touch, are transformed for good.

Leading with Emotional Energy

Understanding your emotional energy is part of this process, but it's how you learn to lead yourself through these emotional energies—particularly the challenging ones—that determines the depth of your emotional power. So, in the chapters ahead, I'm going to talk to you about how to lead yourself in emotionally intelligent ways.

Whether you're a manager leading large teams of people, an entrepreneur leading yourself through the challenges of building a business, a parent leading little lives, an educator leading children's learning, or an individual simply looking to lead a more emotionally satisfying life, this book is for you. I know there's already a lot of great stuff out there about leadership—about the strategy of it, the structure of it, the communications of it, and so on. Our conversation is different in two ways.

First, we will talk about your leadership not as a position but as an overall identity. For our purposes, leadership does not necessarily mean you're a chief executive or have x number of direct reports. It's much broader.

Our definition of leadership is simply this: your ability to use your own energy to influence your own life. This means your leadership isn't only about what you are *doing* between the hours of 9 and 5; it's about who you are *being* across your life. It's about how you steward your life at work, at home, in parenting, in your relationships, and on social media.

Second, your leadership of others relies on your ability to use your emotional energy to lead yourself. In my work, it's common to see leaders of varying types intensely invested in the emotional experiences of *other people.* Managers worry about their employees; parents obsess about their kids; lovers are preoccupied with their partners. However, it's much less common to see leaders consciously reflect on their *own* emotional experiences as a *primary* force that impacts the way they show up in their lives and the lives of others.

Missing the connection between our leadership, our emotion, and our impact renders us less powerful than we actually are. It's not that other people's emotions don't matter in your life. On the contrary, they're tremendously important. In fact, neuroscientific evidence shows that emotions can be contagious. A large scientific literature demonstrates that people neurologically and physiologically synchronize their internal emotional state with the people around them.[5]

While you cannot directly control an emotional state in another person, people *are* influenced by your emotional energy. For example, a parent, frustrated their child won't calm down, can't soothe the child. But when the parent's inner state becomes calm, the upset child rapidly calibrates to this soothing emotional energy. Similarly, a manager, fixated on ways to engage their unengaged employees, feels unmotivated thinking about how unmotivated their team is. But when the manager finds inner inspiration, the unengaged employees attune to the inspiration of their leader.

Our lives break down at the point of our *own* emotional pain—at the point of our *own* negative feelings of stress, fear, inadequacy, and worry. Until you have a situation you *feel* bad about, you do not have a problem. The way you lead your life has so much to do with how you lead yourself though your own difficult emotions—in the decisions you make, the ways you speak, the risks you take, and the connections you keep. When leaders change their own relationship with their own emotions, relationships change and the world rises.

How This Book Will Work

At the core of the neuroenergetics of emotional power are eight neuroenergetic codes. Think of each code as a blueprint explaining how you can harness your brain's energy to create specific improvements in your life and the lives of others.

The first five of these eight codes are for you. The last three codes are for those you lead—your team, your customers, your children, your partner, your social media followers, your friends, whoever. These final three codes will help you more effortlessly attract and inspire the behaviors you hope to see in others.

With each code, I'll give you several examples and reflections because the conversation we're having is not theoretical; it's practical. You will see precisely how to apply these neuroenergetic codes to lead your life in more emotionally powerful ways.

As you may have sensed already, I'll present plenty of ideas in this book that are not conventional. Many will be counterintuitive. With great intentionality, I will ask you to think in ways that may seem outlandish—wrong, even. But the scientific evidence is clear: to overcome experiences of emotional pain we must often do the counterintuitive.

In this book, there will be plenty of stories to illustrate the core ideas. Many of these stories will focus on scenarios at work or at home. But I'll also share examples from other parts of life, drawing parallels that may at first seem out of turn. For example, I occasionally draw on instances of extreme pain—such as combat trauma or childhood trauma. Even if you feel you can't perfectly relate to these examples, I can promise you they have application to some of the more common pain points in your own life. I'll share a range of examples because

I want you to see how, across many divergent situations, there are convergent insights about what the brain is doing. There's a soothing clarity that comes when you know how to work with your challenging emotional energies across a range of variable situations. As you will see, **the brain is the brain is the brain**. And if there's an evidence-based intervention that works at the most extreme forms of human suffering, then it has application to more common circumstances as well.

I'll also draw on the psychology of very complex relationships, such as the parent-child relationship and the romantic partnership as models for how you interact with other people in your life, like your team or your clients. I do this not because I think you are the almighty parent at work or somehow in love with the people with whom you do business. I do this because intimate relationships are the most powerful and complex relationships on the planet. If we can shift relational dynamics in those circumstances, we can do it everywhere else, too.

A brief note about the stories: I've created composite characters. All identifying information has been altered to protect the individuals, but all the stories are based on real people and their real emotional lives.

Finally, I hope this conversation reconnects you to the spectacular energy of your own life. I hope it feels like a homecoming, a remembering that you are—as you have always been—your own most powerful resource.

Get ready for the rising.

PART ONE

Understanding Your Emotional Power

Understanding Your Emotional Power

Neuroenergetic codes for building your emotional power

Before we get into the eight neuroenergetic codes, we need to more deeply define those two categories of energy—emotional pain and emotional power. It becomes much easier to harness your energies when you know precisely what you're looking for, so this chapter will spell out what each of these energies *feels like* and the many ways they manifest themselves in your life. Before you can master them, you must first recognize them. As we work to strengthen your emotional power, you'll see that much of our effort will specifically focus on intelligently handling the energy of your negative feelings—what I'll be calling your emotional pain.

Emotional Pain, Defined

In our conversation, we'll focus less on the slam-your-finger-in-the-door, step-on-a-LEGO kind of *physical* pain. Instead, I'll be talking to you about your experiences of *emotional* pain. **Pain is my all-encompassing word for any negative emotional experience like stress, anxiety, pressure, fear, self-consciousness, struggle, anger, jealousy, disappointment, inadequacy, frustration,**

worry, or embarrassment. I call it all pain because no matter what word you use, the brain processes these sensations in similar ways. This means whenever you say you're stressed, I'm calling it pain. When you're having a "bad day" or you're "on edge," I'm calling it pain. When you're feeling frustrated, resentful, or anxious, it's still pain. Any time you have a feeling you don't like, we'll call it emotional pain. As you will see, distilling countless bad feelings into a single construct is incredibly clarifying—and it's neurologically accurate.

At a high level it works like this: When you experience feelings of emotional pain, it's because a key network in your brain has been activated. This network is called the *frontolimbic circuit*. Imagine it like a neural highway that serves as the connector between key parts of your brain—parts like the amygdala, hippocampus, anterior cingulate cortex, insula, and prefrontal regions. When this circuit is activated, it creates sensations that you ultimately call anxiety, stress, fear, worry, frustration, anger, and so on.[1]

Within the range of feelings we'll call emotional pain, it's important to recognize that we'll predominantly focus on the pain you inflict upon yourself. **Most precisely, we'll be talking about the pain that comes from your willingness to self-betray**. While plenty of pain can be inflicted upon you—this is, for example, what interpersonal assaults and abuse are—a significant amount of pain in your life comes when you abandon yourself. This pain of self-betrayal—the times when you create pain by abandoning or forsaking yourself—is what I call **self-division**.

To understand the pain of self-division, imagine this common scenario: Someone asks you to work on a project that you don't need to do but you feel like you should. You want to say no, thank you, but instead of listening to the truth of your energy, you say yes. When you now have to do the thing that you already didn't want to do, the energy of no is still very much alive inside of your body. You have divided your behavior from your emotion. In this scenario, there's no way you can bring the full force of your energy to your life because you have divided your energy—there's one part of you *acting* in one direction while another part is *feeling* in the exact opposite direction. You are dividing yourself against yourself.

While some pain is indeed inflicted upon you, significant quantities of your emotional pain come from this *self-division*—the moments when *you* deny yourself the things you truly want and need for yourself.

For example, do you ever:

- promise you'll do something for yourself, but then don't?

- want to stand up for yourself, but don't?

- swear you'll hold a boundary, but don't?

- want to speak up, but keep your mouth shut?

- want to connect to people, but withdraw instead?

- want to tell the truth, but stay silent?

In moments like these, you abandon the truth of your own energy—and when you do this, you show yourself you're willing to be your own betrayer. There are certainly scenarios in life that pose clear, acute danger. But that's not what we're talking about here. We're talking about the times we abandon ourselves not because there's any objective danger but because it *feels* too emotionally intense to stay aligned with the truth of our energy.

Because many of your emotional transactions take place outside of your brain's conscious awareness, it's easy to miss the true energetic exchanges that take place. For example, imagine my coworker asks me to do something I don't want to do, or my partner speaks to me in a way I don't like. Both scenarios create negative feelings—like irritation, rage, or disappointment—inside of me. With this energy, I conclude that my partner or my coworker "doesn't even care about me and there's nothing I can do about it." While this is *a* conclusion, it's likely not the most honest one. A powerful question to ask is: Have *I* ever effectively communicated the way I actually feel?

Very often in scenarios like these, the answer is no, and the reason is because we did not know how to lead ourselves through our own painful feelings. Advancing through our own fear, anxiety, and self-consciousness is often so distressing that we would rather hand others the reins of our emotional destiny than address the ways we're abandoning ourselves. Your enduring problem doesn't so much come from what this person did or that person said. It comes from the moments you reject yourself.

On the path to power, there may indeed be conversations you intentionally elect to avoid, relationships you willingly decide to end, or comments you deliberately choose to keep. The purpose of emotional power isn't to respond to every emotional impulse that arises, rather it's to discern the *enduring* truth of what you want.

The idea that we can betray ourselves can be a tough pill for many of us to swallow. I know how alluring the "Yeah, buts" are because I still do them myself. "Yeah, but you don't know what would have happened if I said no to that person." "Yeah, but you don't understand how tough my work is." "Yeah, but you don't understand my marriage." "Yeah, but you don't know my kids." This is an entirely natural, human response. The purpose of our conversation is expressly not to blame ourselves. Quite the contrary: it's to free ourselves. Something surprisingly calming and empowering happens when we recognize that we often act as the main perpetrators of our misery. When we get clear on the ways we cause pain to ourselves, we realize we have a lot of power in its lasting resolution—and this feels like profound relief.

If you want more emotional power, it's also important to remember the central mission in our conversation: we're preparing you for exceptional emotional power—a power that is so expansive it can fundamentally change the way you lead your life. To become the most powerful version of yourself, it is necessary to examine where you are dividing yourself from yourself. Before you can harness your energy, you need to take responsibility for it. *Of course* it would be easier if other people acted in ways that made it easier for you to speak up, hold your boundaries, and be your authentic self. There are probably a million good reasons why it's easier to appease them than it is to refuse to abandon yourself. While that's understandable, it's not leadership.

Take Krish, an entrepreneur who had long dreamed of merging his love of real estate with his gift for teaching. His dream came true when he created a business that offered online training to teach others how to invest in real estate, and hundreds enrolled. But soon, his dream became a nightmare for a simple reason: Krish could not tell people no. One client wanted a refund even though he completed the course three months ago. Krish thought it was absurd, but he offered it. Another person didn't like the format of the course. Krish didn't agree, but he fixed it. Some other clients didn't think it was fair that they didn't have as much real estate success as some of the other clients. Krish thought it was due to their lack of effort, but instead of offering them the truth, he offered them additional services.

While his business looked great on the outside, Krish felt miserable on the inside. He wasn't running his business; his fear of upsetting people was running him. It wasn't simply that he was attentively tending to his customers; Krish was terrified of upsetting other people. He admitted he was so frightened by the prospect of other people's disappointment that he didn't know how to stand up for himself. When Krish wanted to honor his own boundaries but instead overgave to others, he was divided from himself.

To understand if you're dividing yourself from yourself, consider the following:

- When you're exhausted, do you allow yourself to rest—or do you force yourself to "push through?"

- When you want to say no, do you respect your boundaries—or do you choose people-pleasing?

- If your feelings have been hurt, do you honor them—or do you minimize, push down, or ignore them?

- When you want something for which you don't feel entirely comfortable asking, do you advocate for yourself—or do you expect others to read your mind?

- If you're upset and want to talk about something, do you address your desire—or do you avoid it?

- When you realize you've made a mistake, do you speak to yourself in a reassuring way—or do you compound your pain by becoming self-critical?

When you do the latter, you are dividing yourself from yourself. One part of your energy wants to go in one direction (e.g., more rest, authenticity, boundaries) while the other part of your energy behaves in the opposite direction (e.g., overwork, people-pleasing, overgiving). If you divide your energy persistently, you will weaken your energy because your behavior lacks integrity with your emotions. With enough time and after enough self-division, you will find the strength of your energy severely depleted.

Until we understand the principles of neuroenergetics, how to powerfully engineer our emotional lives, this self-division happens largely outside of our conscious awareness. We know we feel bad, but we're confused about the essential source of our bad feelings. We reflexively think it's about how something did or did not happen in our external world, but it's more fundamentally about our relationship with our own nervous system—about who we become in the gap between what we have and what we want.

As we've discussed, you have *a lot* of words at your disposal to describe negative emotional states. For example, *anxiety* and *anger* are just two of the many, and a quick search yields forty-nine synonyms for *anxious* and fifty-two for *angry*.

Regardless of the words you use to describe your bad feelings, your brain treats them all roughly the same. It engages similar neural circuits regardless of whether you say you feel anxious, afraid, irritated, mad, self-conscious, stressed, overwhelmed, or hundreds of others.

The word list below will help you identify emotional pain. Scan the list for some of the things you feel or want to avoid feeling. This is not an exhaustive list, so add any words that are particularly meaningful to you.

WORD LIST

Afraid	Embarrassed	On pins and needles
Agitated	Enraged	Overwhelmed
Angry	Fearful	Pissed
Annoyed	Frantic	Provoked
Anxious	Frightened	Rushed
Apprehensive	Frustrated	Scared
Ashamed	Furious	Sick to your stomach
Awkward	Hurt	Sweating bullets
Bothered	Irked	
Bummed	Irritated	Troubled
Concerned	Jealous	Upset
Despairing	Jittery	Worried
Disturbed	Mad	_____
Distressed	On edge	

It is these sensations of emotional pain—these neurologic zings of negative energy—that are entirely responsible for all the stress and struggle in your life. For example, if you had the highest-stakes meeting of your life, but you were not anxious, you would have no problem. And if the meeting was a colossal failure—if it was so bad that people laughed and gossiped for days—but you did not feel humiliated, you would have no problem. If you then had a conversation with your boss that called into question your very competence but you felt neither embarrassed nor bothered, you would have no problem. And if all of this culminated in your firing but you were not upset, then you would have no problem.

Until you have a bad feeling, you do not have a problem.

The meaning you make out of your life rises on the energy of your emotion. Neuroscientific research shows that emotions bridge the external world to inner meaning. Emotion also modulates cognition.[2] You can't pay attention without emotion, can't imagine without it, can't create without it, and can't make decisions without it.

Previously, scientists understood emotions as automatic, uncontrollable reactions—experiences we simply had to tolerate until, for whatever reason, they relented. But, like all things, science evolves. Now, powerful neuroscientific research shows we aren't victims to our bad feelings, left to submissively endure an emotional pounding until the misery relents.[3] No. We are co-collaborators with our transformable emotional energy—an energy that somehow very much belongs to us and very much doesn't. We all already know we cannot perfectly control our emotions, but when we understand how to work with this energy—instead of just being the passive recipients of it— we participate in our own emotional ascension.

Figure out what to do with your negative feelings and you're playing with radical power.[4] So much of what previously felt too scary, too annoying, or too intimidating is simply no longer a barrier to the life you desire to lead. Moreover, when you figure out how to transform the energy of pain into power, you become a model for those you lead, too.

I understand that pain may initially seem like a difficult topic of conversation. But I trust you will soon see that your pain is not a harbinger of doom. Quite the contrary. Your tough feelings are sacred messengers, offering you profoundly intelligent guidance toward what you truly want. In this book, I'll show you clear step-by-step approaches to work gently but powerfully with a range of your negative feelings so that you can turn your pain into your power.

Emotional Power, Defined

If emotional pain is self-division, then what's emotional power?
Wholeness.

The depth of your emotional power depends on the degree to which you stay whole, and your wholeness depends on your refusal to divide yourself from yourself. The degree to which you refuse to deny your authentic emotions is the clearest measure of your emotional power. Said another way, your willingness to work with your negative emotions is a powerful sign you believe in your wholeness—that *all of you* belongs, even the parts that are challenging or inconvenient.

If pain is the resistance that separates you from achieving what you desire, then power is the energy that allows you to achieve what you desire. Examples of this occur when you:

- Speak up even when it's hard.

- Trust yourself even when others disagree with you.

- Believe in yourself even when you make a mistake.

- Go after your goals even when others tell you they're unreasonable.

- Do what you believe is right even when you're afraid.

- Seek to understand yourself even when others won't.

- Believe in your worthiness even in moments that don't give you clear evidence of it.

Whenever you use your energy to leave one job in pursuit of another, start a new project, improve your relationship, or further develop one of your good ideas, you're drawing on your power to produce a desired effect in your life. To be clear, when I use the word "power," I am expressly not talking about tyrannical behaviors, like control or manipulation of others, that are often erroneously called power. Manipulation and control are technically forms of emotional *weakness*, not power (see sidebar for more).

Emotional power is exceptionally important in uncertain times because it empowers you to stay with your vision even when external forces make it difficult. Emotional power means you have taken the thing that could have destroyed you and turned it into the very evidence of your empowerment.

A Note on the Word Power

The word *power* often carries a sinister connotation. Far too often, we are made aware of traumatizing situations where someone is over-controlling, rejecting, or abusive, and we think of that as a kind of *power*. It's not. That is *the abuse of power*. It's important to be crystal clear: abuse of power does not make a leader powerful at all. In fact, these behaviors represent weakness.

If someone uses their higher-status position to force others to behave in certain ways, this behavioral phenomenon is more accurately called *manipulation* or *coercion*. They are demonstrating the exact opposite of power. The reason anyone needs to force, frighten, trick, or take from others is because they are incapable of doing something themselves or unable to inspire others to *want* to follow their lead.

When leaders lead from an emotionally disempowered place—when they unleash fear and control—others around them sense this emotional energy. Leaders set the energetic tone for their team. While it is possible to frighten people into compliance for *short periods of time*, psychological research clearly shows that these types of punishing energies do not deliver desired results over the longer term. The most powerful leaders on the planet don't demand other people affirm their leadership power. Quite the contrary: they are the ones who help other people remember the depths of their own personal power. It's the empowered leader—not the controlling one—who drives the evolution of their team, their organization, their families, and themselves.

For example, Anthony, the founder of a highly successful startup, was similar to Krish in that he had a habit of saying yes when he really meant no. Each time Anthony insincerely said yes, he felt drained, committing himself to projects and engagements he did not actually think were useful or interesting. Still, Anthony had a reputation for being a star performer in crisis situations.

He came to me because he "didn't feel alive anymore." His energy wasn't very powerful. When I asked him why he kept agreeing to do things he didn't think were useful, he said that it was his job to "make diving catches."

A person cannot work against their own energy and expect greater empowerment. You cannot deny your own injuries and expect greater resilience. You cannot ignore your own exhaustion and achieve aliveness. It was only when Anthony started respecting his own boundaries—calmly telling people he was not available to solve every problem and confidently trusting the competence of his team—that he started to feel more like a leader and less like a frazzled utility player.

I want you to think about emotional power in another way, too. Another word we'll use to describe your emotional power is *worthiness*. Worthiness means you believe in your inherent wholeness—that *all* of you belongs and that *all* of you has value. Not just the happy parts, not just the smart parts, not just the good-looking or hardworking parts. *All the parts belong.*

In neuroscientific terms, the sensations we are referring to as emotional power are generated in the parts of your brain known as "cortical midline structures." Your cortical midline structures include parts of your brain like the posterior cingulate cortex, precuneus, anterior cingulate cortex, and various prefrontal regions. Feelings of worthiness—your sense of self-worth, self-confidence, self-esteem, and self-assuredness—have been demonstrated to show increased brain activations in these areas.[5]

The desire for worthiness is universal because it's the desire from which all other desires flow. You'll never be able to access the emotional power required to express yourself freely, rest when tired, accept abundance, require respect, and allow kindness if you don't first believe that you're worthy of it. The greater your sense of worthiness, the stronger your emotional power.

Connected Energies

At this point, emotional pain and emotional power may feel like opposites to you, but it's not quite that simple. These two energies are inextricably connected, like two sides of the same coin. You can't have one without the other and you don't choose one over the other. You need to understand and embrace both to grow.

Emotions, at the most basic neurophysiological level, are interactions between electrical and chemical energy that show up as sensations in your body. Whether you're anxious, confident, calm, or exhausted, these are all neuroenergetic experiences, brain energies. Strangely, you are your strongest when you put your painful energy to work for you. Just like a jumbo jet is more powerful when it flies on all four engines instead of just one, you are more powerful when you use *all* your energy, even the painful kinds.

I know that it's easy to treat pain as the foreshadower of doom, something to be immediately avoided. But your pain is the precise path to your power. It tells you exactly what you need to feel more whole at this very minute. For example:

- If you feel *exhausted*, this energy is signaling that you want rest.

- If you feel *betrayed*, this energy is signaling that you want loyalty.

- If you feel *rejected*, this energy is signaling that you want connection.

- If you just watched someone achieve an impressive feat and you feel *jealous*, this energy is signaling that you, too, want to do great things.

- If you feel the emotional pain of *boredom*, this energy is signaling that you want more vitality.

Notice that your emotional pain—exhaustion, frustration, betrayal, and so forth—is pointing you in the direction of greater empowerment. It's telling you what you *really* want. Your pain is itself the evidence that greater power awaits you. Just like you cannot know light unless you also know dark, you only feel your pain *because* you remember your power. For example, you only feel the drudgery of boredom because you know you're meant for the energy of vitality. You're only pained by the sting of rejection because you know you're supposed to be powerfully connected. If there wasn't a part of you that didn't remember your bold visions, bright dreams, and big hopes, it would be impossible to be pained by the absence of these things. You already know you want to speak up; you already know the visions inside of you were meant to be expressed; you already know there's more that awaits you. And it's in this knowing—the contrast between where you stand and what you really desire—that's calling you home.

So much of your emotional pain comes from the things you're doing to continually prove your worth. Do you often overwork, overthink, overgive, overcommit, or overcommunicate? If you've ever engaged in any of these painful behaviors, the *only* reason you did this is because you believed that your value was up for debate. Everything on that list is a safety behavior intended, ironically enough, to protect you from pain. Take overwork, for example. Never in the history of humans has someone said, "I'm exhausted, but you know what sounds like a great time? Five more hours of email." And yet, I frequently work with exceptionally accomplished leaders who will not rest even when they absolutely must—not because they don't want to, but because they are terrified to. (There will be more on overworking, overgiving, overdoing, and so on, in the next chapter.)

Throughout this book, I will talk about power—restoring your power, increasing your power, transforming your power, and so forth. It's important to keep in mind our definition of power, which is the strong, positive energy of your worthiness—your wholeness. It's the aliveness that comes when you allow *all* your energy instead of siphoning off the full potency of what you already are. When you claim your wholeness, you become the living standard that shows others how to claim the full power of their life, too.

Pain, Power, and Other People

When we talk about emotional pain and emotional power, you'll notice these energies are mostly focused on you, the individual. What about those around you? As a leader—a manager, entrepreneur, parent, partner, educator, or content creator—don't you have a powerful responsibility to extend empathy, inclusion, authenticity, transparency, and other powerful energies to the people who depend on you?

Yes, you do. But this book deliberately focuses on you first. You cannot powerfully help other people with their negative feelings until you first know what to do about your own.

- How can you empathize with other people's pain when you ignore your own?

- How are you going to meaningfully include people when you don't even feel like you belong?

- How are you going be honest when there are parts of yourself you still deny?

- How can you hear others' pain when you don't even listen to your own?

- How can you be patient with others when you feel crushed by the frenetic pace of your own life?

You cannot give what you do not have.

We will talk about other people more in the second part of the book, but for now understand that people want to be treated kindly, fairly, and honestly by you because your leadership influences their emotional power—their beliefs about their own worthiness. When you treat your people in ways that remind them of their wholeness, you remind them of their power.

With this understanding of emotional pain and emotional power, you're ready to learn the neuroenergetic codes that will help you rise to new levels of empowerment. Know this: Your emotional energy is here to work for you. Your work is to collaborate with it. The rest of the book, through the eight neuroenergetic codes, offers you a clear system for strengthening your emotional power.

Code 1:
Expand Your
Emotional Power

How to transform your emotional pain into emotional power

I f you've been avoiding your negative feelings, it is absolutely not because you're weak. It's because your brain is working magnificently well. Just like when the doctor hammers your knee and your leg reflexively kicks, your brain reflexively avoids pain that rattles it. Of course, this reflexive response to pain has profound advantages, allowing you to survive a dangerous world, often with little thought at all.

But there's a galactic difference between surviving and thriving. Neuroenergetic code 1 shows you how to overcome your brain's automatic pain avoidance response by taking those feelings of stress, fear, and anxiety to catalyze a massive expansion in your emotional power.

At first, you might think working with your painful feelings sounds miserable. After all, pain is your brain's distress call—the neurologic sensation designed to reactively get you out of a situation as quickly as possible. However, I can tell you that when done wisely, working with your negative feelings becomes a transformative opportunity in your life. I say this so confidently because, for many years, I've worked with people who have risen from the depths of despair by developing a new relationship with the feelings they swore they could not feel.

I also know it's a fact of neurobiology. The most effective, scientifically supported forms of behavior change are fundamentally predicated on people transforming their relationship with the feelings they've been avoiding.[1]

Some forms of avoidance are already crystal clear to you. For example, if you burn your hand on a hot stove, you will immediately—without any conscious thought—yank your hand away to avoid more pain. The same is true for instances of traumatic emotional pain. Imagine you had a terrible car accident on a bridge that left you emotionally traumatized. There's a good chance your brain would convince you to avoid the bridge in the future: you might take a new route, cancel your trip entirely, or ask someone else to drive.

While the examples about bridges and burns are valid, they are low-hanging fruit. Simply understanding those obvious manifestations of pain will be insufficient to deliver you to the full expression of your emotional power.

Let's instead turn to more insidious forms of pain avoidance. Note the ones you recognize:

- You want to tell someone what you're really feeling, but you're too *afraid*, so you *avoid* it.

- You are really excited about launching a new product, but you'll be *embarrassed* if no one buys, so you *avoid* it.

- You have been wanting to start a new creative project, like a podcast or a book, but you're *insecure* about what other people might think, so you *avoid* it.

- You're having trouble with one of your employees, who keeps making mistakes, but you're too *frustrated* to talk about it calmly, and *afraid* of how they may react to your criticism, so you *avoid* it.

- Fill in your own example here: _____

In all of these examples, your brain is trying to avoid pain by avoiding the situation.

The travesty of this type of pain is that the full range of your leadership—the depth of your energy and the breadth of your visions—won't be decided by you; it will be determined by tough conversations, embarrassing circumstances, and difficult people.

Think about the items you just noted. I want to show you how avoidance traps a massive amount of untapped energy inside of you. For example, if you want to create a podcast, but the stress associated with being judged stops you, then all the power contained in the energy of your creativity remains locked inside of you for as long as you avoid this expression of your creativity. To recognize how much of your energy may be trapped in your emotional pain, complete this three-part exercise. Note all that apply:

1. Do you spend any time each day:

   - *worried* what other people think of you?

   - *irritated* by what people keep asking of you?

   - *scared* you did something wrong?

   - *afraid* to speak up even though you really want to?

   - *panicked* that you never have enough time?

   - *anxious* you're not living up to other people's expectations?

   - *stressed* you've upset other people?

   - *overwhelmed* by tasks you feel you must do?

   - *terrified* if you really lived your life as you desire you would be rejected?

2. Then, do you compound your original pain by feeling additional pain about your original pain? For example, are you:

   - *exhausted* from all that worry?

- *depleted* from persistent people-pleasing?

- *frustrated* by why you keep overreacting to situations you logically *know* aren't actually a big deal?

- *mad* at yourself for caring so much about what other people think?

- *disappointed* that you can't trust other people as much as you would like?

3. Then to try to create a sense of security, stability, or safety, do you engage in what I call the "overs?" For example, do you:

- *overthink* to try to find the perfect solution?

- *overanalyze* to try to understand what people *really* think about you?

- *overcheck* your email, social media, or phone to make sure you don't miss anything or make a mistake?

- *overgive* to keep people from getting mad at you?

- *overdeliver* so you don't disappoint people?

- *overwork* as a strategy to avoid getting overwhelmed and to "stay on top of things"?

Paradoxically enough, the "overs" are actually your brain's attempts to keep you out of pain. Take Daphne, a self-proclaimed and exhausted people-pleaser. "I've tried to stop overdoing it so much because I'm miserable," she lamented, "but I always feel guilty and afraid that people will be mad at me if I say no." In this example, you can clearly see that the core energetic impulse of Daphne's overgiving isn't about helping other people; it's about protecting herself from her own painful feelings of guilt, fear, and worry. Her strategy of overgiving is one of self-protection. The thinking goes: if she can just give enough, she can protect herself against the threat of other people's anger and disappointment.

What I want you to see is that there's a colossal energetic difference between giving and overgiving; between thinking and overthinking; between committing and overcommitting; between working and overworking. As soon as you enter the "over" state, your brain becomes energetically depleted. *You* have ignored your own brain's cues that you are giving too much, thinking too much, working too much, or doing too much. Through your own acts of self-division, you put yourself in a state of pain.

The cost of constantly ignoring your pain is the life you actually want to live. Until you're willing to acknowledge the truth of your energy, your full potential will remain trapped inside you. In my experience, there is no more worthy task—no greater act of self-devotion—than to examine the truth of your whole energy.

Neuroscience is unequivocally clear: your chronic painful feelings are draining your energy. They steal how good you feel, how well you think, and even how long you live.[2] When it comes to the energy of your negative emotions, you have two choices: you either remain trapped in perpetual avoidance of them, or you work with them to fuel an expansion in your emotional power.

As I lay these two choices before you, you might naturally ask, "Why can't I choose option C—the one where I avoid pain entirely and it all goes away?"

Because you can't.

Can't you just teach me how to get rid of my pain?

The truth about pain is you can never eradicate it; you can only transform it. There is no energy on the planet that can be destroyed. For example, when water turns to air, it's not gone; it's only transformed. Because your negative emotions are, quite literally, a neurobiological energy, they're governed by the laws of physics. Perhaps you recall from your high school science classes something called the law of conservation of energy that tells us that "energy cannot be created or destroyed." It also tells us that while energy can't be destroyed, *it can be transformed*.

If the energy of pain in your life could have been destroyed, you would have eradicated it a long time ago. You have a brilliant mind that routinely tackles difficult problems. You may regularly solve tough business problems, troubleshoot intense parenting dilemmas, and engineer complex social events. Your own life has shown you that you can resolve plenty of challenging situations in your life. If you could have "solved" your emotional pain—your repetitive feelings of stress, anxiety, or insecurity—you would have by now.

Instead, like a bad game of whack-a-mole, the situations change, but those same painful feelings keep popping up. Sure, some pains are fleeting—like being aggravated when someone cuts you off at a stop sign. But that's not what we're talking about here. We're talking about the chronic bad feelings that keep appearing in your life—the ways you're *persistently* stressed, *consistently* on edge, or *repeatedly* annoyed.

Neuroenergetics helps you see your negative emotions as an energy. As such, your work isn't to destroy your painful feelings, but to transform them. This responsibility to transform your pain is great, because if you don't transform it, you'll transmit it to the many people who look toward your leadership. You pass your pain on to your team when you act short-tempered, frustrated, or cold. You pass it on to your children and partner by being distracted, unattuned, and impatient. Worst of all, you pass it on to yourself.

The biggest injury from our untransformed pain is often the continuous wounding of ourselves. Consider Sheila, a successful entrepreneur, who founded two eight-figure businesses, one in the physical product space and one in consulting. On paper, Sheila had it all. Two booming businesses and three healthy young children. But Sheila was a bear to be around. Her staff complained that Sheila was critical and volatile: the product launch wasn't good enough, the new branding wasn't good enough, the inventory wasn't good enough. In this energy, her staff turnover was excessively high, which only exacerbated Sheila's anxious volatility.

In my work with Sheila, she admitted that she was difficult to work with but explained, "No matter how hard they think I am on them,

I'm a million times worse to myself. I grew up in a home where criticism was the leadership strategy." Sheila shared a story about the time she won the state golf championship. "The first thing my mother said to me after I received my medal was 'You looked like shit on that fourth hole.'"

"You know the first thing I thought when I hit seven figures in my business?" Sheila asked. "That it was shit because it wasn't eight."

As we worked together, Sheila saw the way pain naturally moves. She began to see her strained relationships with her team as an energetic mirror for her self-punishing relationship with herself. What comes out of us is based on what is already inside of us. Because Sheila was in pain, she transmitted pain. For Sheila—as for all of us—the healing work is to reconnect to our emotional power, which is our inner sense of wholeness.

Expand Your Edge of Emotional Power

Your edge of emotional power describes the amount of energy your nervous system can hold while you remain connected to your power. It's the outermost amount of sensation you can tolerate before your brain becomes imbalanced—before your brain is dysregulated by negative sensations and you become emotionally unsteady. Right now, you have a set point of how much painful energy you can endure before you become too triggered to respond powerfully. For example, you may think you're perfectly fine, but then suddenly you lose your emotional center when your partner makes a specific comment, when your mother speaks in a certain tone, when your kids behave in a certain way, or when you read a certain comment on the internet. In these moments of emotional reactivity, your brain loses its balance.

This happens in one of two ways. Your brain either becomes *hyper*aroused or *hypo*aroused. When you're hyperaroused, the sensations in your body feel too big. You may feel too anxious, too angry, too overwhelmed. Your heart may be pounding, your hands may be sweating, your face may be flushing, your thoughts may be racing.

Hypoarousal is less well-known but equally problematic. It's a dys-regulated posture of the autonomic nervous system in which your emotional state is *under*active. If you have been emotionally hypoaroused, you may have felt numb, flat, depleted, depressed, blah, sluggish, zoned out, or disconnected.

In both states—hyperarousal and hypoarousal—you're disconnected from your emotional power, unable to access the energy that allows you to pay attention, be creative, soothe yourself, and make strong decisions.

The point right before you enter a reactive state is your current edge of emotional power. Practically speaking, it explains, for example,

- why you trust yourself in some situations but doubt yourself in others

- why you thrive in certain roles, but shrink in others

- why you're willing to assert yourself in an email, but too scared to do it in person

- why you're certain you have a fantastic idea until a more powerful person signals even slight confusion

- why you can stay calm until someone says just the wrong thing

Becoming more powerful by eradicating this energetic edge is a false option. The laws of physics do not let you destroy energy. When ice expands to become water and then water expands to become vapor, nothing is gone; it's just changed. In fact, as ice transforms into vapor it becomes—literally—more energetic and expansive. Similarly, as you work to transform the energy of your pain, you also become more energetic and expansive.

Your goal is not to try to get rid of pain. Your goal is to try to expand your edge—augment it so you can hold more neurologic energy. When you expand your edge, your brain will stay centered in the same situations that previously would have caused it to become hyperaroused or hypoaroused. As you expand your edge of emotional power, things that used to make you quite anxious, stressed, or overwhelmed still exist; they just no longer perturb you. When it comes to a tough circumstance in your life, you really have only two options: run from it or become more powerful in the face of it. This neuroenergetic code will help you do the latter.

There are two ways you expand your edge of emotional power:

- Pick a more powerful pain.

- Hold your emotional shake.

Pick a More Powerful Pain

If you find yourself chronically feeling bad, experiencing the same problems over and over, chances are high you're stuck because you've been seeking the perfect solution. But you don't need a perfect solution; you need a powerful one.

Perfect solutions don't exist, because they're predicated on the total absence of pain's energy, which is scientifically impossible. Instead of trying to eradicate your pain, what you want to do is first clearly understand the pain you feel and then pick a more powerful pain—a pain that will ultimately make you stronger because you're able to hold more emotional energy.

Let's use an analogy that will make this clear. If you're trying to get physically stronger, you go to the gym and lift more weight. At first, twenty pounds may be the edge of what you can comfortably tolerate. But you decided your goal is to get stronger, and you know you must pick a more powerful weight. Let's say you work long enough that you're now able to lift forty pounds. Clearly, you've gotten stronger.

But here's the thing: When you're able to lift forty pounds, it's not that twenty pounds no longer exists. In fact, you will forever have to lift twenty pounds in order to lift forty—twenty is inherently part of the forty. Twenty pounds didn't get easier; you got stronger.

To see how this relates to your emotional life, let's apply this logic of picking a more powerful pain with your partner.

Let's imagine your partner is upsetting you because you feel that you have to excessively take care of them—you do their laundry, cook their food, do all the grocery shopping, take care of the kids, pay all the bills, and even remind them about their own appointments. You feel more like a parent than a partner. You continue to do this work for them, all the while hoping they'll change. Maybe you've had multiple conversations with them about how their behavior bothers you; maybe you've displayed your sadness to show them how their behavior is hurting you; maybe you've even made snide remarks—all in the hope that they will change *their* behavior to deliver you from *your* painful feelings. If you could get them to change, this would be your perfect solution. But as one of my academic colleagues used to say, "Crap in one hand and wish in the other and see which one fills up first."

You may now decide it's time to choose a more powerful pain: you are no longer willing to do this much work on behalf of your partner because you feel like your own self-respect is waning. You know, though, that when you do this, you will have to face their threatening emotions. Chances are high they will be mad at you. They also may be hurt, asking you why you don't care about them anymore. They might start to respond to you in passive-aggressive ways. Maybe, your worst fear materializes and your new boundary leads to the end of the relationship.

I realize this can sound devastating. But don't panic. It's clarifying—steadying, really—to realize that there is absolutely no scenario in which you magically avoid all pain. Now, ask yourself a power question: *Which pain do I choose?* Do I choose the pain that comes from feeling disrespected, unappreciated, and parental? Or do I choose the pain that will likely come when I attempt to expand into a relationship with more self-respect, partnership, and intimacy?

These are not empty, moralistic questions—faux reflections where the choice is already self-evident. These questions are so powerful precisely because they orient you to the truth of your life, which is this:

in a life where there is no pain-free option, which pain do I genuinely choose? This level of honesty is a total power move.

In the former caretaking scenario, you already know the precise pain your current situation offers simply because you've been living it for a while. It's totally OK to stay in this version of a relationship if this pain is genuinely acceptable to you. But if you desire to expand your edge—to meet the natural and stressful resistance that comes with change—you have the chance to build the relationship you've been dreaming about. Maybe with your current partner, maybe with a new one but, above all, with yourself. This change, like any change, comes with the pain of the unknown.

Note that in the weightlifting example, you don't lift twenty pounds one day and then lift forty pounds the very next. You make these changes in an incremental way. To apply this logic to the example with a partner, you don't have to summarily leave your relationship. Perhaps you start by simply refusing to remind your partner of their personal appointments and you hold this position until you can tell your edge has expanded. You'll know your edge has expanded to hold more energy when you no longer feel feelings of anxiety, fear, and worry when you don't remind them of their appointments. Your brain—just like your muscles—*will* acclimate to hold this new "energetic load." Next, you take on the bills and repeat the same process. Next, the kids and the cooking and so on.

At each phase, *you* are empowered to evaluate how the situation is working for you. Do *you* feel sufficiently respected? Do *you* still desire further change? If yes, in what way? It is true that sometimes the people around us refuse to change. Even so, you are now empowered with new data about the old patterns that *were already harming you.* Maybe you realize you, in fact, are comfortable continuing to caretake your partner in the ways you have been doing—and now, armed with this new perspective, you caretake your partner willingly instead of resentfully. Great.

Or maybe you realize that you can't have a meaningful, intimate relationship with another person so long as you feel you're not respecting yourself and you ultimately decide to begin couples therapy or even leave the relationship.

Regardless of what you decide, it's soothing to realize that if you want to engineer your life in emotionally powerful ways, there's really only one mistake you can make: continue doing the same thing *you already know is hurting you and expect a different result.* Your emotional power expands at the edge of your old behaviors.

Meg's story

I worked with Meg, a global VP of a multibillion-dollar company, and the youngest person ever to hold her role. She was slated to soon become the next CHRO. She credited much of her meteoric success to being a "consensus-based leader." While this characterization was true to a degree, Meg came to realize that "consensus" was often code for "people-pleasing."

If a meeting was elective, Meg would be there. If you sent an email at midnight, Meg would have a response before you woke up. If the CHRO wanted a report by Friday, Meg would deliver it by Tuesday. "If one more person tells me how 'responsive,' I am, I'm going to freak out," she told me.

Although she could clearly articulate that her success was due to her sharp intellect and rich experience, she *felt* that her continued success relied on her willingness to "not disappoint people." She said she had been pleasing people for as long as she could remember. In other words, the sheer energy of her people-pleasing was creating a ton of pain. Each time she overgave, overexplained, or overdelivered, Meg felt her energy drop. The more she did it, the more exhausted, stressed, and resentful she became. Eventually she had reached her emotional edge, often feeling hypoaroused—totally depleted and numb to a life she once loved.

Working together, we decided to help her expand her edge and become more emotionally powerful by picking a more powerful pain. The more powerful pain she chose was self-respect.

If you're thinking *What in the world?! Self-respect isn't painful!*, I want to assure you that it absolutely is. If it were pain-free to be self-respecting, Meg—like everyone else in the world—would already be self-respecting. The price of true self-respect is indeed great. To be self-respecting, we must be willing to deeply honor our own energy *even at the cost of other people's approval.* In the moments we prioritize our own respect, we stop living our lives in accordance with other people's preferences and start living in alignment with the truth of our own energy. We honor our sacred yeses and heed our sacred nos. For many of us who attribute our very success and safety to being pleasing to others, the decision to become deeply self-respecting is utterly terrifying. To minimize this truth is to hinder our effectiveness at achieving change.

Meg swore that all she wanted in her life was more self-respect—the strength necessary to effortlessly hold boundaries and confidently make choices. However, as Meg prepared to say no more readily, her pain increased. She became more nervous, more anxious, and more guilty than she had felt before as a people-pleaser. She wondered what balls would get dropped and who would be mad at her if she stopped overdoing.

Through our work, Meg saw two options before her. She could continue with the devil she already knew—the familiar pain associated with people-pleasing. To remain with this pain was to already know its cost. She had already amassed years' worth of evidence in the form of self-resentment, exhaustion, fights with her husband, and missing important moments in her kids' lives, like baseball games and dance recitals.

Or Meg could pick up a heavier emotional weight than the one she had been lifting for all this time. This would be a less familiar but more powerful pain. It would be the pain of uncertainty. The brain dreads uncertainty (and we'll talk about this in depth in code 4). Meg was truly fearful of what would happen to her reputation if she stopped looking at her email at 6 p.m.—would people think she was slacking? She worried what would happen if she said no—would people think she was uncooperative? She was scared of being passed over for a promotion—would people think she was unworthy?

As she became more committed to adopting the powerful self-respect she knew she wanted, all these painful fears initially *increased*. Understanding neuroenergetics, the way emotional energies move, helped Meg immensely. If she didn't understand her negative energy, she could have erroneously interpreted spikes in her fear, stress, and anxiety as evidence she was on the wrong path. The *opposite* is true. By understanding that emotional pain reliably accompanies expansion in emotional power, she was able to use her sensations of emotional resistance as evidence she was finally heading where she wanted to go.

There's a relief that comes when you realize what your brain is reflexively doing. Meg's initial feelings of painful distress were her brain's misplaced attempts to help her. The brain's primary goal is simply survival. Even though Meg's people-pleasing was making her miserable, her brain already had plenty of evidence to show she could survive feeling bad about herself, fighting with her husband, and missing her kids' lives. What her brain did not yet know was if it could survive the uncertainty entailed in a bold new range of behaviors.

It's only when we get intentional enough about the emotional energy in our lives that we can even see the panic in situations long enough to transform it. Remember: your brain is so good at helping you avoid pain that you often cannot immediately see the actual source of the circumstances that are making you miserable until you choose to be deeply intentional with your energy.

Expect any transition to a more powerful emotional posture to take some adjusting. When someone works up the courage to work with the energy of their pain, I've noticed that they inevitably will start to rationalize or minimize their pain. For example, Meg's CHRO held a meeting in which she invited some of Meg's counterparts, but not Meg. Meg *knew* that the reason she was not invited was because the meeting was not directly related to her work and Meg had begun to ask that she not be invited to non-essential meetings. However, Meg, thinking aloud, spontaneously said to me, "I don't know, I just feel excluded—like they don't care if I'm there or not." Once she realized she said it, she scrambled to take it back, "I mean, I know they weren't rejecting me; I didn't mean it like that."

But her emotional system absolutely did mean it like that.

Meg needed to allow the whole truth of her emotional energy if she wanted to access greater emotional power. If you have never held a boundary before, the holding of a new boundary *will* initially feel like terror. So what. To change, you must understand there is an other-worldly difference between *being* in danger and *feeling* in danger. Your tough feelings are just that—feelings. A few intense zing-zing-zap-zaps that your nervous system is *designed to handle.* Your nervous system packs 150 million years of evolutionary power. You are built to handle hard.

Going after what you want in your life *is* powerful precisely because it *is* painful. It's so natural to admire people who really go after their dreams because, even if we don't consciously state it, we all recognize the deep vulnerability and terror associated with risking so much for the things we desire so deeply.

There's something to understand about the way your brain processes pain that is quite astonishing: it is often the anticipation of pain that is more painful than the pain itself. (We'll talk more about this in neuroenergetic code 4.) But for right now—in this code about expanding your emotional power—it's important to remember that it's your *fear* of pain that is often more painful than the *actual* pain you experience.

Meg ended up achieving the self-respect she had been longing for. I took her through the following four-step process to help her expand her edge of emotional power by picking a more powerful pain. I'll now show you how to do this, too.

Exercise

1. Pick a More Powerful Pain

First, I asked Meg to identify her deepest emotional desire by asking herself: What do I truly want? Examples include:

- I want to feel freer.

- I want to feel more self-respecting.

- I want to feel more excitement.

- I want to feel more self-expressed.

- I want to feel more confident.

- I want to feel safer.

- I want to feel more unconditionally worthy.

- I want to feel more relaxed.

In Meg's case, her deepest desire was to feel more "self-respecting." For you, answering this question may take probing. Often our initial answer is not deep enough. Meg's initial desire, for example, was about getting other people to behave a certain way. There was one colleague Meg had an especially hard time holding boundaries with and, subsequently, Meg was extra people-pleasing to this person. Understandably, Meg had fantasies about "what if this person left the company?" When we began, Meg was seriously contemplating switching companies. Through our work, Meg ultimately discerned that her deepest desire was to feel more "self-respecting."

If you feel pulled to say something nonemotional, like you desire a promotion, a bigger team, a new business, or a salary increase, you have not gone deep enough. Remember: emotions give meaning to all things in your life. You want a promotion, for example, because it makes you *feel* something. Maybe it's more freedom, more safety, or more excitement. Identify the emotional energy, not the vector to it.

2. Process Your Most Powerful Pain

Processing your pain will help defuse it. To do this, describe the most catastrophic thing that *could* happen if you pursued what you truly wanted. There is a doomsday scenario in your brain that is blocking you from going after what you truly want in your life. Nearly always, this block is a nebulous feeling—a free-floating sense of doom—and not a clear, logical ordering of events. The expansion of your emotional power starts when you put some linearity to the chaos of your painful feelings.

Precisely name all the potentially awful things that could happen if you pursued your desire. *Play this out to its most painful conclusion.* The conclusion will almost always be entirely illogical. When you start to clearly articulate the catastrophic conclusion, it will sound absurd— because it is. And in its absurdity, you will be tempted to intellectualize against it (e.g., *This is ridiculous,* or *I know I'm being too dramatic,* or *This won't actually happen,* or *I know they weren't really trying to reject me*). Do not intellectualize against the imagined catastrophe of the more powerful pain or the exercise will not work.

When Meg thought about her barriers to becoming more self-respecting, she described it as a flow of catastrophic energy that went like this: I disappoint people by telling them I can't do something, and the painful floodgates open → My boss starts to realize I'm no good → I get fired → I can't find another job → I can't support my family → We lose our home → I am totally unable to protect myself and my children → I am humiliated in front of everyone I ever knew → We are ruined forever, unable to recover.

Of course, as soon as she clearly articulated the catastrophe associated with her more powerful pain, she *knew* the statistical likelihood of her ending up homeless, unable to protect her family, and forever ruined was infinitesimally small. While she was tempted to intellectualize against it, the truth is this fear was very much alive in her emotional system. You must work with the energy that is present in your nervous system in order to release it.

Because your brain's singular function is your survival, if there's an unprocessed energy of danger, you will stay stuck here in the more familiar pain. To free yourself from your emotional pain, there's something counterintuitive to understand. The brain readily remains in chronic emotional pain because it is often the *chronicity itself that allows your brain to calculate it's a pain you can survive.* For something to be chronic, it must be familiar. Even though Meg was in significant pain, zapping all her energy through relentless people-pleasing, her brain had tons of evidence that people-pleasing wouldn't kill her. Even though Meg felt miserable, her brain knew it was safe enough to survive. What her brain did not yet have evidence for was what would happen if she started to expand beyond this suffocating cycle by choosing a more powerful pain.

3. Rate Your Pains

Take a piece of paper and draw two columns. On the top of the left column, write "Familiar pain." (For a visual of this exercise, see table 1.) In this column, list every painful thing you have already endured as a function of your current behavior. Again, be highly specific. For example, Meg wrote, "Missed Elisha's basketball game for the third time this season" and "Working almost nightly until 1 a.m."

On the top of the right column, write "More powerful pain." Then fill this column with the data you generated from step 2 ("Process Your Most Powerful Pain"). For example, Meg included in this column things like "End up fired and unable to ever find a new job" and "Totally unable to protect myself and my children."

Next, rate each entry on a scale of 1 to 10 of how *likely* you think it is to occur, with 10 being extremely likely and 1 being highly improbable. Do this for both the "Familiar pain" and "More powerful pain" columns.

This is a bit of a trick exercise because the "Familiar pain" column should be entirely 10s. In other words, each of these entries represents something you *already know* makes you miserable. In Meg's case, she already knew that she was in pain from missing three of her son's basketball games and working until 1 a.m.

Since you already know the answer, you might be tempted to skip rating your familiar pain. Don't. This step is very powerful. Having all your data right before your eyes is a powerful way to separate clear evidence from the nebulous sense of free-floating doom, and it's a motivator to help you decide how to empower yourself.

Table 1 includes a sample from Meg's list.

TABLE 1

Meg's pain ratings

Rating	Familiar pain	More powerful pain	Rating
10	Missed Elisha's basketball game for the third time this season	End up fired and unable to ever find a new job	1
10	Working almost nightly until 1 a.m.	Totally unable to protect myself and my children	1
10	Have spent no 1:1 quality time with husband in months; now fighting regularly	Am humiliated in front of everyone I ever knew	1
10	Maeve at bedtime said, "All Mama does is work."	Am ruined forever, unable to recover	1

4. Discern Which Pain You Think Contains More Energy for Your Expansion—and Then Pursue That

With all your data before you, you can now make an empowered choice. Remember, there is no perfect way of avoiding pain. It's a phantom option, an illusory choice. Once you're clear that there is no perfectly pain-free option, it becomes much easier to pick a more powerful pain—the route that makes you stronger rather than keeping you stuck.

The steps of processing your pain, rating your pain, and discerning your pain are all predicated on neuroscientific evidence. Emotional pains that block us from pursuing our dreams are usually vague. People have long recognized that talking about their pain or cognitively approaching pain by giving it a numeric value can lessen its burden.

Recent neuroscientific advances have shown us why. Your painful emotions are generated in subcortical regions of your brain that include structures like the amygdala. In brief, your brain's subcortex contains parts of your brain that are older and more primitive. Words, however, are an evolutionarily newer function of the brain and are produced in cortical, not subcortical, regions of your brain. Therefore, when you put your feelings into words, doing so activates cortical parts of your brain—regions like the right ventrolateral prefrontal cortex—that then help calm hyperactive subcortical parts of your brain, like the amygdala. Similar processes are involved when you assign a numeric rating to a nebulous feeling.[3]

In sum, if you want a more empowered life, your work isn't to eradicate your problems. It's to upgrade them. By using this four-step process, your emotional energy becomes undeniably stronger.

Hold Your Emotional Shake

Now that you understand how picking a more powerful pain can expand your edge of emotional power, let's discuss the second strategy, "Hold Your Emotional Shake."

Let's go back to the physical strength analogy. Imagine that presently you can only lift twenty pounds and your goal is to get stronger. You know exactly what you need to do: start working with heavier weights. You decide to go straight to thirty pounds. You begin to lift it, but quickly your muscles start to shake. Do you panic in this moment—freak out, assume the shaking means imminent dread, and flee from the gym never to return?

No.

You understand that the shaking is *itself the evidence of your increasing strength.* In fact, for plenty of people who work out, the shaking is satisfying—enjoyable, even—because it is the clearest signal that they are accomplishing their goal of getting stronger.

It's the same for emotional strength. When you want to get stronger, you need to meet a more intense level of emotional resistance. And when you do, change happens quickly.

Daisy's story

Daisy was an early-career professor. She had recently completed her PhD and was exceptionally prolific, publishing in scientific journals. Daisy combined sharp analytical skills with strong storytelling abilities in her research on parenting, and her work started receiving increasing attention in the nonacademic world. She was fielding interview requests from large radio shows, TV program, and podcasts. While Daisy was initially excited, she soon became highly anxious.

When she came to me, she described spending sleepless nights writing out, rehearsing, and trying to memorize answers to innumerable interview questions. She explained, "When I give speeches at scientific conferences, I know exactly what I'm going to say. I have my deck, I have my data, and I have my speech in front of me. But on these live interviews, who knows what they're going to ask?" When Daisy was giving a prepared speech, she felt like she was in control, but when she was having an impromptu conversation, she felt out of control.

Like many high performing leaders, Daisy had a perfectionist streak and, while it was easy to see the value of that style earlier in her career, she was now starting to see the pain of it. "Now that I'm getting more attention, I'm terrified of saying something stupid—and it just spirals. I imagine myself saying one minor thing that's not precisely right and, suddenly, I've totally discredited all my research and my entire life's ruined." She was ready for a change: "I know I need to stop because I'm making myself sick with all this overpreparing."

Daisy had to choose between two pains. She could stick with the pain of her "overs"—the overpreparing, overplanning, overthinking, and overworking. Or she could choose the more powerful pain of self-trust. If you're tempted to say there's nothing painful about self-trust, I want to assure you there absolutely is. If it were pain-free to be self-trusting, everyone would already be self-trusting. In Daisy's case, she knew that she knew her research—she was the one who had created it! But perfecting a canned speech and trusting your deep intelligence in the moment are two different leadership skills. To quit the pain of her perfectionism, she needed to come alive in the energy of the moment. To do this, she would need to "hold her emotional shake."

For Daisy, her emotional distress manifested physically. When she showed up to interviews unrehearsed, she literally shook. Her hands trembled, her legs felt wobbly, her voice quivered, her heart fluttered, and her thoughts raced. Just like someone whose biceps shake as they lift more weight at the gym, Daisy was in the throes of her own emotional shake. But here's the amazing thing. She held her shake for five interviews—five! After that, the shake was gone. As Daisy held herself through her emotional shake, her nervous system habituated to a new level of emotional power. Now the very interviews that had, just moments ago, terrified her, excited her. Daisy reported, "When I first came to work with you, I thought I would never give another interview again, and now I'm actually having fun."

If Daisy would have responded to her emotional shakiness as a sign of imminent danger—if she had canceled the interviews or had just given memorized responses—she never would have reached this new level of emotional power.

You can expand your emotional power by holding your emotional shake using a simple two-step exercise. Here's how.

Step 1. Create an "emotional weight" list

Rank five to ten activities by the distressing "shake" they cause you. Any activity that causes you to feel shaky can go on your list. It could be a tough conversation with a team member, a bold decision you've been avoiding, or an annoying call to your cable company. Don't think of the substance of the activity, but the *emotional intensity it produces inside of you.* As we discussed with Meg, the part of the brain that gives rise to your painful feelings does not rank things, organize them, or sort them. Thus, ranking your pain by the shake it causes is already part of your solution.

In Daisy's case, her list looked like this, ranked in increasing order according to the level of the pain (represented by a number from 1 to 10 applied to each activity):

2 = show up with answers to multiple questions memorized

7 = show up entirely unrehearsed to a mid-range podcast

8 = do a series of impromptu live events on my social media account where I field questions from the audience

9 = show up entirely unrehearsed to a national radio interview

10 = show up entirely unrehearsed to a national television interview

Next, you're going to pick one of these activities to train on. Only you know the level of resistance that's right for you. People tend to start this exercise around a level 7 or 8 resistance. Just like Goldilocks, you want a level of resistance that is neither too easy nor too hard, but one that is just right. A 10 would be too much, and a 2 not enough.

Step 2. Continue to do the chosen activity until the shake no longer pains you

You can't go to the gym once and expect lasting change. You need to work repetitively with your emotional resistance to get stronger. Repetition is the master of the brain. Know, though, that your goal is often not to get the shake to zero. It was not Daisy's goal to have zero level of hyperarousal.

Go back to the gym: When you get strong enough to lift forty pounds, your muscles still hold tension as you lift twenty. If you're going to be leading an important conversation or making a big decision, there will always be some degree of arousal: your pulse will quicken and your posture will change. This is good news. You do not want to be overly relaxed on an interview to the point of drifting off. Recall that Daisy said she started to see impromptu conversations as "exciting" and not "dreadful." Excitement is still an actively energized neurologic state. Our goal for you is to calibrate your energy to its optimal level.

This repetitive approach to your emotional resistance—the idea of repeatedly holding your shake until your emotional power changes—reflects one of the most neuropsychologically informed, evidence-based approaches to overcoming pains like anxiety, fear, stress, and worry. Think of the scariest horror film you've ever seen. The first time you watched that movie, it was painful. You were terrified. But now imagine that you rewatch it three times in a row. Your levels of pain would decrease substantially. What if you then rewatched the movie five times? Ten times? Fifteen times? By the fifteenth time you watch the same movie, the scenes that just moments ago tormented you would transform into something so predictable they would bore the hell out of you.

This is called "habituation," a well-studied neuropsychological phenomenon that simply means you repeatedly expose yourself to something that initially pained you and, after repeated exposures, your brain learns—through the evidence you present to it—that the thing it thought was dangerous is not dangerous.[4] This process releases you from the pain cycle. The thing that previously caused you to shake painfully is now the thing that has become the evidence of your new-found strength. You have expanded your edge of emotional power by holding your shake.

Connecting the Two Strategies

I want to connect the underlying neuroenergetics of the two strategies—picking a more powerful pain and holding your emotional shake—for you. More important than the mechanics of these two strategies and exercises is the underlying energetics. You might think that the successful end game for Meg or Daisy would be to have no fear while giving a specific interview or saying no to a specific colleague. Certainly, these situational outcomes are a bonus—but there's a more fundamental goal.

The central goal for Meg and Daisy—as it is for you—is to create a new relationship with the energy of your emotions across *all* situations. Remember, all emotions are just electrical impulses in your brain—a bit of zap, zap, zing, zing, crackle, crackle. That's it. That's all they are. When you learn to see them as only energetic sensations and not some harbinger of imminent doom, your whole emotional landscape suddenly opens up.

As you learn to tolerate feelings you previously avoided, you will likely find that the sensations you wasted so much energy avoiding lose their heat. And when you understand how to work with the underlying mechanics of negative emotions, your emotional power grows.

Different Places, Separate Spaces, Same Brain

You saw how both Meg and Daisy had spent significant time trapped in punishing pain cycles. However, when they found the right process for their pain, their lives evolved quickly. There's a great myth that change takes a long time. When you work at the right level of pain, the rise to your empowerment happens fast. You'll see this clearly now in the story of James, a combat veteran with post-traumatic stress disorder, or PTSD.

To share the story of a combat veteran with PTSD might seem too dramatic, like I'm suddenly comparing apples to furniture. But I can't stress enough that neurologically similar forces are at play even if the details are completely different. The brain is the brain is the brain. And the general strategies that allow us to transform our pain apply quite consistently across situations.

When James came to see me, it had been more than a decade since he saw the battlefield. He's still earnest as he describes his early enthusiasm for joining the military in the immediate aftermath of 9/11. But his nostalgia quickly fades as he recalls in vague sentences and fragmented thoughts how his patriotic aspirations became an enduring nightmare after a raid went wrong.

At first he's suspicious of therapy and wryly asks, "I guess we now blame everything on my feelings?"

"No," I say, "In here, we'll spend most of our time blaming your mother."

He laughs and we get comfortable. I ask him, "What have you been doing to cope with your trauma?" He rattles off a list: he doesn't go into crowded spaces or public places; he can't stand the news, so he doesn't watch that; he's not able to work because he's easily triggered and frequently gets into altercations with coworkers; he mostly refuses to drive; and worst of all, his wife recently left because he wouldn't engage with her or the kids.

In a word, he's *avoiding*. James is suffering tremendously, suffocated by a life where he now avoids too much.

The logic here is universal—whether you're talking about stress in your corporate job, anxiety from public speaking, or trauma from a war zone—the brain is reflexively wired to avoid anything that reignites the specter of pain. Good news for James is the neuroscientific evidence is very clear about what to do in situations like this.

"The best science for PTSD says do the *opposite* of what you've been doing," I tell James. "In other words, we're no longer going to avoid reminders of what happened in battle. Instead, we'll collect evidence to see if you really need to be so afraid of what you've been afraid of. To collect this evidence, we'll talk about your trauma in highly specific detail. And we won't just talk about it once, but over and over. And we won't just talk about it in session, but we'll record you and then you'll go home and listen to it repeatedly each day."

Testing the safety of the strange idea, he asks a series of ostensibly innocent questions: What if he can't handle it? What if he starts crying and can't stop? What if the nightmares get worse? He's particularly concerned about vomiting while talking about his trauma, so he wants to know, What if he gets sick?

I take the trash can from under my desk and place it next to him. "If this works, I think we can both agree that a little puke is a small price to pay."

Note how James—just like Meg and Daisy—uses "what ifs" to play out *imaginary worst-case scenarios*. Note also that it's the very fact they entertain these imagined scenarios that has locked them into suffocating emotional holding patterns. There is no expansion here. There is no power here.

There is no rising here.

To change, James must collect evidence that services his emotional expansion—he must pick a more powerful pain and hold himself through the emotional shake that will follow. I take this chance to remind him that there's great news: He's already done the hardest, bravest thing. He survived the *actual* trauma. The war is over. He is home. The trauma treatment is challenging, yes. But we can change this; he can do this. His face softens, his shoulders drop slightly, and he decides to do it.

At week twelve, he walks into my office and abruptly says, "Doc, I can't take this anymore."

"Sit down," I say, "What's been going on?"

He leans forward in his chair and shakes his head, "I cannot listen to this thing one more time," he says while pointing at his phone that holds the recording of him talking about the war.

"Why not?"

"Because every time I listen to this thing, I fall asleep. I can't stay awake. Dull. As. Shit."

James had done it—and he had done it in a breathtaking span of twelve weeks. The trauma that had tormented him for more than a decade—the memories that made it so hard for him to be in public, drive, or be present with his family—was now so boring it lulled him to sleep. It was indeed a radical act of transformation. He had expanded his edge of power.

. . .

Telling you these stories of human transformation still brings tears to my own eyes and chills to my own body. Witnessing such staggering acts of bravery, rooted in profound self-devotion and deep hope for a brighter future, has shown me that there is so much freedom in our pain. We hemorrhage so much of our holy energy, frenetically avoiding the things that make us feel bad. But in what I suggest to you is the greatest paradox of human existence, those painful feelings—the ones you swear are destroying you—are here to set you free. And when you realize this, your emotional rising is well underway.

Code 2:
Build Your Power Pattern

How to harness the brain's
pattern-detection abilities

I n the last code, I showed you how to increase your emotional power by picking a more powerful pain and holding your emotional shake. While these approaches will work well in any situation, I want to offer you something even more powerful than a situation-by-situation approach. In this code, I'll show you how to *build your power pattern*. Your power pattern is the very frame that will allow you to respond in emotionally powerful ways across a range of difficult situations in your life.

Patterns are vitally important to your life because of how your brain works. Your brain is the most powerful pattern-detection machine in the world.[1] The environment around you is teeming with an impossible quantity of information: sights, sounds, words, articles, opinions, news cycles, and more. If you had to think about each piece of information that entered your brain, you would be utterly paralyzed by the sheer quantity of it all.

So, your brain moves you smoothly—effortlessly, even—using patterns to predictively determine your next course of action. Without much conscious thought at all, your brain is running its constant calculus: say these things but not those things; do these things but not those things; act in these ways but not in those ways. Approach this. Avoid that.

Pattern detection is so central to your brain that areas like the insula, amygdala, cerebellum, premotor cortex, basal ganglia, and thalamus, as well as parietal, temporal, and frontal areas are all involved.[2] All of that simply to say: it's hard to find a part of your brain *not* involved in predicting what comes next in your life.

In some ways, this prediction ability is astoundingly helpful, and in others, it can lead to painful dysfunction. Many scientists, including myself, use a well-validated face processing task that speaks to the power of patterns. Inside an fMRI scanner or hooked up to an EEG, people are shown pictures of various human faces. Some of the people in the scanner have no mental health conditions, and some have conditions like generalized anxiety or PTSD. Some of the faces they see are happy, some are fearful, some are angry, and some are neutral.[3] People with preexisting conditions like anxiety disorders report the neutral faces as threatening, whereas people without such conditions do not. The brain activity of the anxious participants corresponds with their self-report, showing activations in brain regions responsible for fear and threat detection, like the amygdala.[4]

In these experiments, everyone is shown the exact same faces—there is no debate about who saw what. This then raises a powerful point about preexisting patterns that extend beyond the experiment: Is it really that the situation before us is *objectively* too dangerous or scary? Or is it that the brain routinely finds what it *predicts* should be there?

Note the hopeful message here. If you need the situation to change before you can feel any greater sense of empowerment, your chances for success are low, because many situational factors are indeed outside of your control. But if your greater empowerment lies in changing your own internal patterns, then relief is very much within your reach.

OK, now let's build on that. Can you make out anything in the figure on the next page?

This image, inspired by the work of neuroscientist Dr. Lisa Feldman Barrett, looks like a meaningless blob.[5] There appears to be no clear pattern. But notice that, in trying to figure out a pattern, you're giving this task substantial cognitive effort. You're dedicating cognitive resources like attention, working memory, visual memory, and problem-solving and, despite your best attempt, you're still unable to solve the pattern.

Turn to the end of this chapter; what do you see in that image?

A clearly recognizable object, right? A bit of contrast and texture helped you find the pattern. (When you see this image in color—it's brown and white—the effect is even more immediate and pronounced.) It's great that you see the clear pattern, but that's not the most important takeaway here. Look at the blob again. The most important point is this: You cannot unsee the animal. Now that your brain knows the pattern it predicts should be there, it continues to see it. In other words, your brain's predictive abilities are so good that your brain will still cling to subtle and ambiguous hints about old patterns *even when the pattern is no longer meaningfully there*. The pattern has objectively changed. It's empirically less clear, but you're still superimposing the pattern you learned *then* in a way that is changing what you perceive *now*.

The power of your patterns cannot be overstated. They govern nearly everything about the quality of your life. For example, whether you generally think entrepreneurship is exciting or dreadful; marriage hard or easy; or alone time soothing or scary has everything to do with your patterns. Studies from neuroscience and psychology demonstrate that two people can experience the same event and yet have drastically different interpretations. These differences in "objective" reality are explained, in part, by individual brain differences, the fact that each person's brain is filled with distinct preexisting patterns that lead them to make different interpretations about meaning.

The most extreme example of this fact occurs in trauma. Much of my scientific research examines neurocognitive and neurobehavioral responses to trauma and predictors of PTSD. You might be surprised to know that the strongest predictor of how people respond to the trauma is not the trauma itself, but who they were before the trauma.[6] Even in the most painful circumstances in our lives, it's our underlying patterns that play a powerful role in our response to pain.

In this neuroenergetic code, I will show you how to powerfully work with your underlying patterns to steady you in almost any storm. For this work to stick, I want to first clarify why attempts to change our lives commonly fail. It's because people take on change at the level of *specific situations*. Imagine the following scenarios:

- A manager, worried that his team is underperforming, thinks: I just need my team to land *this* deal.

- A parent, frustrated with their kid's academic performance, thinks: I just need to get my kid to do well on *this* math test.

- A spouse, worried that her partner won't agree with her, thinks: I just need my spouse to agree with *these* plans for our upcoming summer.

In each of these examples, the focus is on achieving something in a *specific situation*. If you try to create change at the level of your situation, the attempt will ultimately not work. There is no sustainable power here because your underlying pattern—the pattern that gave rise to your situations in the first place—remains intact. As long as the underlying pattern retains its power, it will continue to repeat. Even if you break your pattern in one situation, chances are high it will pop up again in the next. To powerfully change your patterns, you must tackle them at the level of *time* and *emotion*. I'll show you why.

Let's start with time. Complete this easy pattern: Apple. Apple. Apple. [Fill in the blank].

What word do you think comes next? Obviously, it's Apple.

The only way any pattern detector can work is if the past is superimposed on the present. The reason you know the answer is "Apple" is because you used past data to fill a future blank. While this speedy pattern-detection ability is great if you're looking for fast answers, it's terrible if you want to make an interesting fruit salad. More relevant to your life, if your underlying pattern is not expansive enough to hold possibilities beyond your current pattern, you will block your own evolution.

In part, the Apple example is so simple because it's devoid of emotion. The meaning in your life is determined by the emotions you have about it. Your emotions about the big things—your relationships, your team, your career, your kids—do not spontaneously emerge in a vacuum devoid of past attachment. Instead, what you feel in any present moment is both tethered to and sustained by your historical patterns. For example, how do you typically feel when people depend on you? How do you typically respond to pressure? How do you typically feel about the future?

Your patterns explain why, for example, when you get a new job, find a new relationship, or move to a new city, you may feel upbeat at first—the sensation that true change is here to stay—but then quickly return to feeling how you always felt. While novelty may give you an initial spike in emotion, the pattern-detection abilities of your brain eventually take over and superimpose their "old" patterns over your "new" life.

For example, my client Sam plowed through five jobs in three years. Each time he left a job, he lamented that the job was too painful—that the demands were too stressful, the coworkers too annoying, and the customers too demanding. It was when he started to look for his sixth job that he discovered a powerful insight. Although he had changed situations multiple times, his complaint was the same: he was too stressed out. Sam realized that across diverse situations, *he* was the only common denominator. It was this realization that no amount of external situation-fixing could change his internal energy. That's when Sam began to lead himself in a new way and finally found the relief he was seeking.

The pattern detection abilities of your brain are fundamentally invested in predicting your survival. *Everything else* is secondary. Do you know what the surest test of survivability is?

Familiarity.

If you have been here before—no matter how bad you felt—it's familiar enough that your brain is certain you can survive it. This is good for surviving, but deeply problematic for thriving. Your brain does not calculate familiarity by the *facts of a situation*. Instead, familiarity is measured by the *feelings you feel about a situation*. For example, plenty of times, you've walked into a totally new room with a totally new crowd of people and you, in an instant, determined if this place felt safe to you or uncomfortable. It had almost nothing to do with situational specifics of the room—the location of the room, the temperature of the room, or even the people in the room. It had to do with *the familiar feelings you felt about those things*.

Your patterns are powered by your emotions. Just like Sam, if it feels familiar to you to be stressed at work, then you will recreate the pattern of stress at work. If it feels familiar to you to be disappointed by people in relationships, then you will recreate the pattern of being disappointed in relationships. If it feels familiar to you to think other people's behavior is your responsibility, then you will recreate the pattern of making other people's behavior your responsibility. To break this depleting cycle, you need to build your power pattern.

Exercise: Build Your New Power Pattern

I call the new pattern that will upgrade your old, painful patterns your "power pattern;" it is designed to empower you to overcome the familiar but ultimately unsatisfying patterns that are currently detracting from the promise of your life. You'll build your power pattern through three steps.

Step 1: Design it

To design your power pattern, you need to first understand what you're building. This pattern is a holy frame, the sacred scaffolding designed to hold your whole life. Your power pattern needs to be big enough and beautiful enough to hold the full boldness of your life. Think of the creation of your power pattern the way you would think about building the house of your dreams—a home so magnificent it takes your breath away. It's so perfect you can hardly believe it's yours. This is not the time to be pragmatic or small.

This is the time to build a masterpiece.

Be deeply intentional. You want this pattern you're about to design to be bold enough and expansive enough to hold every single one of your triumphs and your tragedies in a way that leaves you continuously empowered. Much like your dream house, the vibe you're going for here is, "Oh wow! I get to live my whole life in this energetic space!"

Yes, yes you do.

As you work to intentionally design your power pattern, first be honest with yourself and assess what pattern you typically grasp for when you fall into pain. For example, if you were trying to land a major business deal or buy a home and the deal fell through, notice if you typically think something along the lines of "See, nothing works out for me." Or when you're significantly hurt in a relationship— maybe someone said they were going to do something and didn't—note if you typically think: "I knew it; no one can be trusted," or "The only person I can really depend on is myself."

These are the patterns that are currently giving your life meaning. *It's the edge of your pattern that will constrain the power of your life. You will not be able to sustainably hold on to any feeling that you have not created a pattern to hold. If your underlying patterns cause you to reject things that feel too beautiful, too successful, or too intimate, then you will reject them even when they show up in your life.*

As you think about the ways in which you repetitively fall into pain in your life, notice that it's likely because your patterns are too small for the role you're trying to play. To use our earlier example, if you have a pattern that generally says, "The only person I can really depend on is myself," then this pattern will hamstring your ability to build a large business, run a large team, or manage a bustling household. You can't run a larger operation if you can't rely on others. It may seem counterintuitive, but the bolder your pattern is, the *safer* you become because it creates more space for you to hold all your energy—the pleasurable kind and the painful kind.

Design a pattern that makes you feel incredibly expansive—more possible, more confident, and more beautiful than ever before. To do this, think of a word, a blurb, or a simple sentence that makes you feel so empowered that if you actually embodied the energy you intended with those words, there would be almost nothing in your life you couldn't handle.

Here are some samples I've witnessed in working with people building a more powerful version of themselves:

I am my greatest work of art

I am already worthy

I already have what I need

It's not failure; it's feedback

I can't run out of options

I am ahead of my time

I am powerful enough to be misunderstood

I am on this planet to lead this work

I am my own hero

I am already ready

I can't really get it wrong

I can't mess up creativity

I'm not chasing the answer; I am the answer

To succeed, I surrender

Life happens for me

This pain is already making me more powerful

Everything contributes to my powerful evolution

My life is a brave experiment

There's always a way

I'm exactly on time

Joy in the body

All is already well

Infinite possibility

To the edge of creation

I was born worthy

My greatest work is to nourish myself

Divine love

To see the power pattern in action, consider the case of Anabelle. A true renaissance woman, Anabelle held an MD and a PhD in molecular biology and worked at an Ivy League university. She was a lifelong dancer, and her undergraduate degree was in fine arts. Since she was a little girl, Anabelle had big dreams of being a healer who combined medicine and dance. As an adult, she had earned elite credentials so that she could combine cutting-edge science with the wisdom of healing arts, like dance.

Anabelle began an organization dedicated to her innovative interpretation of health care. While her organization was growing, Anabelle did not achieve success at the speed she wanted. Mostly, she was frustrated that others weren't supporting her organization as much as she had hoped.

When she came to work with me, she was ready to quit her dream. Anabelle and I talked about what leadership meant to her. We paid close attention to the underlying pattern that was giving rise to her desire to quit. Anabelle realized that at its deepest core her central pattern was: "No one understands me." It's OK to be frustrated when you don't get what you want at the speed you want. But you must think powerfully of your interpretation of these things if you want to be able to hold on to your dreams when the storms set in. Anabelle had a big dream inside of her that could ignite anew if she had a power pattern.

Anabelle was a pioneer—no one in the world was doing exactly what she was doing. All she needed was a frame that would help her take the sting out of some of the inevitable resistance that comes when one is truly a pioneer. For her power pattern, she chose "I am ahead of my time."

Step 2: Test it

Once you design your power pattern, it's time to take it into the real world and stress test it. You want to ask: Does it offer you a sense of empowerment in situations that previously triggered you? In Anabelle's case, the power pattern represented a new dawn in her leadership. No longer did she feel unbearably rejected by other people's resistance. For her the evolution from "No one understands me" to "I am ahead of my time" was so significant that she stopped interpreting other people's resistance as a rejection of her and instead saw it as evidence of her being on the cutting edge. Armed with a new pattern, she now saw herself as a visionary, whose work included leading others to ideas they did not yet understand.

Step 3: Repeat it

If you're more than a year old, chances are you've been operating off your patterns for quite a long time. Be gentle with yourself. A great way to express that gentleness is through graceful commitment to repetition. Patterns only exist through their repetition, and repetition is the master of the brain.

The great news is that your brain is neuroplastic, meaning that it is capable of throwing out old patterns that hurt you and bringing in new ones that heal.[7] What's so great about the promise of repetition is that it allows you to free yourself from the pressure of "having to immediately get it right." Repetition generously offers you ample opportunity to experiment with the work of art that is your own sacred life. If you've been running your life on patterns that don't help you much, no big deal. You're never behind time because the thing about this life is it gives you plenty of opportunities to repeat again and again.

In Anabelle's case, she really started to understand that her power lay in her *emotional energy* as opposed to each *individual situation*. With this awareness, she paid close attention to *any time* she started to feel like "no one was understanding her." When the emotional energy zapped, she breathed into her resistance and gently urged herself to soften her grip on an old story that was only harming her.

As her grasp on the old pattern loosened, she was able to reach for the promise of something more. Now, when she received another grant-funding rejection, when her academic colleagues seemed confused about her work, when she watched her peers get yet another promotion, and even when her mother expressed disappointment in her career choices, Anabelle reminded herself that if she was truly ahead of her time, then she couldn't judge her success by the hallmarks of conventional opinions and traditional systems. When her mother asked her for the umpteenth time "why she couldn't just get a normal job at the hospital like her cousin Douglas," she began to release her rage. Instead of exasperated ranting at her mother, she now focused her energy meditating on great pioneers of the past. She was particularly inspired by Thomas Edison's persistence. He worked on *at least* three thousand different theories to develop an electric light.[8] "What were those conversations like with *his* mother?" Anabelle wondered, "No, ma! I don't care about the other 2,999 times. I'm telling you: This time's the time!"

. . .

No matter where you are in your life—no matter what's happened to you or how behind you believe you might be—there's always space for your evolution. Always. If you look at your life as a constant work-in-process, a dynamic work of art that is *forever* evolving, you start to free yourself from the oppressive clutches of time. In my work with my clients and patients, I often remind them that we are on a journey with no destination. When you take the pressure of the destination away—when you release the frenetic sense that you need to be anywhere other than where you are—something profound happens: you find the freedom to engage fully with your life exactly as you are, precisely where you are. And this is the place—the only place—where lasting transformation ever takes hold.

In this image, you can clearly see a snake.

Code 3:
Harness Your
Emotional Energetics

*How to work with your deepest
emotion in the toughest situations*

The last code, build your power pattern, showed you that your brain is a pattern-detection machine. So, what powers this machine?

Your emotions.

Emotions are, quite literally, your first language—the way you first communicated your desires the moment you were born. They're primitive, raw, unapologetic zaps of neural energy that we feel, physically. And in their power, our emotions can be confusing. For example, we *know* the comment was just a joke, so why do we *feel* hurt? We *know* the email wasn't a big deal, so why do we *feel* annoyed? We *know* the thing our boss, partner, or friend said wasn't that threatening, so why do we *feel* anxious?

One of the main reasons it can be difficult to resolve your negative emotions is because you're confused about the true source of your pain. It's a pretty easy sell to say that no one's particularly emotionally powerful when they're feeling especially confused.

The purpose of this neuroenergetic code is to dramatically expand your emotional power by showing you how to work with one specific emotional energy that's singularly painful in your life. It's an emotional energy that's so powerful it's at the root of nearly all the emotional pain you experience.

That emotion is humiliation.

As we discussed earlier, there is a tremendous range of ways to describe your emotional pain: anxiety, stress, fear, frustration, rage, worry, and irritation are but a few.[1] While these are all painful in their own ways, humiliation is generally more painful than the rest. This neuroenergetic code shows you how to specifically work with the energy of humiliation.

The Pain Tree

The energy of humiliation is powerful and universal, giving rise to many painful situations in your life. To show you how this energy works, I created a model called the pain tree. I'll show you how it works and then show you how to apply it by walking you through an example with a client.

The pain tree represents emotional pain in your life. Like all trees, it has roots, a trunk, and leaves.

Of course, you want a tree that is healthy and full of vitality. But there are times when your tree is not doing well. You know your tree is struggling whenever you find yourself feeling bad. To figure out what ails you, let's examine the tree.

The leaves

In this analogy, the leaves represent every individual *situation* in which you experience any negative emotion. For example, if you have an upcoming deadline that's stressing you out, that's a leaf. If you see a photo on social media that makes you jealous, that's a leaf. When Michelle disagrees with you, Danny doesn't deliver what he promised, your kid melts down in the grocery store, and your spouse offers unsolicited tutorials on proper ways to parent, these are all leaves.

All of us tend to spend a lot of time focused on leaves. In the pain tree, the leaves represent *situational specifics*—the details of particular events in your life. When your feelings have been hurt, you reflexively describe the specific details of the *situation*: "You said it would be done by Tuesday." Or "It was only supposed to take a half hour but it's already been three hours!" Or "You promised the client the deliverables would be there yesterday." Or "You always say you'll empty the dishwasher but you never do." You get the idea.

Of course, we live our lives situation by situation, but your lasting power does not lie in your situations; it lives in your emotions. When you're in pain, it's easy to point to the situations in your life as the cause of your pain, but *your situations are never the cause of your pain*. Your emotions about your situations cause your pain. Again, this is not semantics; this is neurobiology. If you did not have any painful energy from a situation, you would have no problem. Painful situations are necessarily the result of painful emotion. When you privilege the situation over your emotions, you paradoxically give away a tremendous amount of your power.

Because your brain is a pattern detector, you have been patterned to pay more attention to the details of the events than how you *feel* about them. But when you focus on situation after situation after situation, you waste your entire life lost in the leaves. Listen: you do not have to be an arborist to realize that you do not help a sick tree by going leaf by leaf to make it better. This is lunacy!

You must leave the leaves.

You now draw on your own bravery to do something pattern-shattering: stop thinking about situational specifics and start thinking about the more essential emotional energetics that exist beneath your situations.

The trunk

Leaves only *reflect* the health of your tree. Your trunk is more essential to the actual health of your tree.

In the trunk of your pain tree, situational specifics are removed. Instead, there are only emotional energies, the neurological sensations that electrified you during your situation: the zaps of anger and the zings of frustration. The trunk contains one specific emotional energy: anger. As I've explained, I don't care much about the semantics you use. You might describe your own angry energy as being annoyed, mad, frustrated, enraged, furious, irritated, impatient, and so on. It's all the same energy.

Angry energies are paradoxical. They project the illusion of strength—they appear to be powerful but often pack no punch at all. As a neuropsychologist who regularly treats people who have endured horrific traumas, I see how chronic anger, an extremely common and understandable emotional reaction, quickly becomes a position of emotional stuckness. People get angry again and again in an attempt to provoke some type of change and yet their lives do not improve. Focusing on anger can't really drive the change you're seeking because it's not the source of your pain. Fear is. The only reason you get angry is to protect something you're *afraid* of losing.

If someone breaks into your home, of course you would be enraged. Your rage activates you to defend against someone taking your property or hurting the people you love. But you cannot be angry—whether it's minor irritation or full fury—unless you're scared about something first. Anger is very often preferable to fear because anger feels like protection whereas fear feels like exposure. But targeting angry emotions alone won't elevate your emotional power.

Consider the case of Jesse. When Jesse came to work with me, she was particularly irritated with a coworker. While Jesse complained that she found this coworker "annoying" and "hard-driving," she admitted that the coworker was well-liked by most people. Jesse was stuck in an angry, irritable loop until we looked deeper. As we did, she started to realize that the energy of her anger—her irritation and annoyance—was shielding her fear. Jesse's coworker was bright and productive, and Jesse realized she was afraid her coworker would outpace her and receive a promotion before Jesse did. It was only when we identified the accurate emotional target that we were able to shift Jesse's situation in ways that empowered her.

Consider these examples in your own life:

- Do you ever get *angry* when someone disagrees with you? Chances are good that you're *afraid* that you'll look incompetent, like you don't know what you're talking about, and you're scared people won't think you're good enough or smart enough.

- Do you ever get *frustrated* at your kids for misbehaving in public? Chances are good that you're *afraid* their behavior may embarrass or reflect poorly on you.

- Do you ever get *angry* at your partner in a way that is disproportionate with the "offense," such as getting extremely frustrated when they don't do something the way you wanted? It's the deeper *fear* of not being understood by the one person on the planet who's supposed to understand you that typically triggers these types of angry interactions with our partners.

Whatever it is, your anger is there to defend against what you're more essentially afraid of losing. This then begs the very powerful question: What is beneath the anger?

The roots

As we just discussed, fear. Fear lives in the roots of your tree. Letting go of anger and admitting there is a more fundamental fear requires a tremendous amount of courage. However, when I work with clients who bravely drop the shield of anger and journey into their fear, they typically make a common mistake and assume that the situation *caused* their fear. For example, people say:

- I'm afraid if I speak up about this situation at work, my boss will criticize me.

- I'm afraid my spouse won't agree with the plans I made for the weekend.

- I'm afraid that if I launch this specific program, no one will buy it.

- I'm afraid if I make this specific social media post, people will think I'm stupid.

- I'm afraid of my team thinking I'm not smart enough in this meeting.

- I'm afraid of doing too much work on this project.

- I'm afraid of losing this job.

Notice how those statements all represent an insidious return to the leaves. The second you start *situationally* labeling the fear—when you say, "I'm afraid of losing *this* specific job," "I'm afraid *this* specific person might say *this* specific thing," "I'm afraid *these* specific people will do *this* specific thing"—you have left the supreme power of your emotional energy and inadvertently gone back up to situational specifics of the leaves.

Your root fear is *never accounted for by any particular situation*. Instead, your root fear is an energy. Most precisely, your root fear is about the energy of humiliation. It's the sensation of humiliation—the way that energy makes you feel in your body—that ignites most of the painful situations in your life. Humiliation is so powerful that you don't even need to *be* humiliated to be activated; you just need to be afraid that you *might* be. Synonyms of humiliation include unworthiness, shame, embarrassment, awkwardness, guilt, and self-consciousness. Just as with synonyms for pain, they all describe the same energy. Whether a person says they are feeling humiliated or ashamed, the brain is doing the same thing. I will use the word humiliation because, in my experience with clients, it's the most potent word.

This word has such a strong energy that it may even be hard for you to read. Notice if you have any knee-jerk reactions to the mere suggestion that there may be things in your life that have humiliated you. You might want to quickly scratch the idea, to say there is nothing in your life that's humiliating you. However, because the energy of humiliation is so devastatingly painful, your brain will always be vigilant about even the slightest hint that you could possibly feel humiliated—not that you *will be* humiliated, but that there's a slight possibility you *could be* humiliated. In other words, humiliation—as well as the fear of humiliation—is the root energy that innervates your entire pain tree.

Think of something mildly embarrassing, awkward, or uncomfortable that happened to you. I'll share an embarrassing moment of my own. I'm short and so I've never liked podiums. I remember once, as I stood at the podium in preparation for a speech, the event organizer—who was wearing a mic—asked me to stand up, and I had to say: *I. Am. Standing.*

Of course, the room erupted in laughter, and I was pretty sure this was a totally legitimate reason to move to the woods and live off the land.

These instances we call embarrassing or awkward fly like warning shots, threatening to pierce our sense of self-worth. As I stood behind the podium, the audience's laughter weakened my grip on my worthiness as I thought to myself: *See, you are a joke.*

We all endure these kinds of feelings, some bigger, some smaller. But when these painful feelings hit, we are often left unmoored—adrift in a flood of what can feel like boundless panic. In our frenzy, we grasp for the most obvious thing we can see: the leaves. But your redemption lies in your roots. The way to overcome these feelings is to reach underneath your situational specifics and fully address the energy giving rise to them. It is a supreme act of power to both acknowledge these painful feelings and to work with them.

The clearest place for me to show you how angry emotions, like frustration and contempt, really mask the more vulnerable energy of humiliation is in couples therapy. When couples begin treatment, they are eager to share their list of grievances about each other: He never listens. She's too controlling. He's a slob. She sleeps too much. He yells too much. She needs therapy.

Underneath each of these harsh criticisms is a tender longing for connection. When one partner says to another something exasperated like, "Can you ever take your face out of that phone?" this is often a call for connection—albeit an emotionally unintelligent one.

What the partner usually means is, "Hey, I really miss you. Do you miss me, too?" But to ask that question means to be vulnerably exposed. Your brain, ever sensitive to the slight insinuation of humiliation, computes that outright humiliation is a very real possibility. What if, your brain warns, after such an exposed invitation, your partner rejects you—grunts at you, refuses to put the phone down or, worse yet, tells you they do not miss you. It is therefore a defensive strategy to protect against a potentially humiliating rejection from our partners by beginning the interaction from a defensive posture: "Hey, stop staring at your phone!"

But people mirror our energy, and instead of getting our partners to put down their phones and lovingly turn their gaze toward us, they usually respond in equally defensive ways, tersely stating "No," giving an exasperated eye roll, or snapping, "Mind your own business." The powerful, healing shift in the couple begins when people recognize that beneath their contentiousness is the tender underbelly of worthiness and connection combined with the universal fear of being rejected and thus humiliated.

When both people in a couple are willing to work honestly with the truth of their energy, the transformation starts to happen at lightning speed. But it's only when people are powerful enough to work with this painful energy that they can change their situation.

I know—professionally and personally—how much humiliation hurts. That's what makes us so desperate to avoid it. But if you immediately run from your energy of humiliation, you can never defuse its painful influence on your life. There are two central reasons you want to clearly understand how the energy of humiliation works.

First, unaddressed humiliation is so dangerous because it alone destroys the integrity of the good self. In other words, *it is only humiliation that can take your power.* Sadness doesn't take your power; anger doesn't take your power; frustration doesn't take your power; fear doesn't even take your power. It's only humiliation that destroys your belief that you're powerful—or worthy—enough to hold *anything* good: love, attention, compliments, safety, rest, wealth. When you're unable to hold meaningful amounts of these things, you'll live a very painful life. And this is precisely why your brain is so vigilant about fighting off anything that *might* humiliate you.

Second, there's something humiliating about admitting you're humiliated. Most people are either unaware or unwilling to admit that another person contributed to their sense of humiliation. As someone who routinely works with teams, couples, and families in tremendous pain, I can tell you that humiliation energizes all kinds of "downstream" painful situations that—to the untrained eye—look like they have nothing to do with humiliation when they have *everything* to do with it.

For example, an executive team made what it considered a small reorganization to their HR team. No one got fired, and no one had to change locations. The main shift occurred as employees were reorganized into new teams and new offices. You can imagine leadership's surprise when what they thought was an inconsequential move flipped the place upside down. One of the leaders said, "People lost their minds. You would have thought somebody died. Everyone was so upset—and over nothing!"

As I spoke with the employees, it was clear it wasn't nothing. They described the experience as a surprising and poorly communicated change that felt "disrespectful" and "unsettling." One employee said, "Did it not occur to them to talk to us? It's like we don't matter at all."

What energy does a lack of mattering always produce? Humiliation.

If these executives had understood the power of emotional energetics—the predictable ways in which emotional energies move through relationships—they could have predicted and avoided this stressful situation. Note that by examining the emotion first they could have ameliorated the situation.

Maybe you still think I'm making too big a claim, stating that humiliation is the root emotional pain. To illustrate this clearly, I'm going to offer two examples that are intentionally quite different: employee engagement and combat veterans.

Let's start with employee engagement. One of the best predictors of employee engagement is not salary, bonus, title, or benefits. It's whether employees believe they matter to their job and that their job matters to them.[2] But why would it matter so profoundly if a person feels like their job is meaningless but they are, for example, well paid?

It's like this: If I work a job that I conclude does not matter to me, then I'm wasting my time and energy doing something I decided was meaningless. The more I give away the holy days of my life to something I already determined was meaningless, the more I work against the value of my own life. I have self-betrayed—divided myself from myself by forcing myself to *do* something *I* felt was unworthy. The word humiliation means to reduce someone's value or worth. If I'm the one persistently working against my own well-being, then this is a humiliating act of self-betrayal. My own actions are reducing my own worth. No amount of money can make up for the inner pain that accompanies significant self-betrayal.

Humiliation is so universal and powerful that I regularly see it throughout my work. When I first started working with veterans, I assumed their worst fear would be a fear of death. Seemed logical. But that's not what I heard. Instead, I heard across veterans, across wars, across experiences that the worst fears were:

- Being the one who screwed up the mission

- Being the one whom others couldn't depend on

- Being the one who was the weakest in the group

In other words, they were reporting that the fear of being humiliated scared them more than death.

Remember, your brain's number one function is to protect you—and your brain is damn good at its job. Your brain does not wait until you *are* humiliated to take defensive action. It's hypervigilant, patrolling the perimeter of your life looking for anything that might, could, maybe, possibly, sorta, kinda be even a tiny bit humiliating to you.

This hypervigilance is a safety strategy—but one that comes at a steep cost. Paying vigilant attention to anything that *could* humiliate you requires a tremendous amount of your brain's finite energy. So long as your brain devotes colossal amounts of energy patrolling the perimeter of your worthiness, you cannot use that energy to expand into a more powerful version of yourself.

Something incredible happens when you see this energy of latent humiliation not as something there to destroy you, but as something that can be used to liberate you. When you work wisely with the energy of humiliation, it elevates you toward your peak power—your unconditional worthiness. And when you touch your unconditional worthiness, you access astounding emotional power.

Dave's story

Dave, the senior leader of a large tech company, learned to work powerfully with the energy of humiliation. Dave had a reputation for intolerance of even the smallest mistakes. He came to work with me after feedback revealed that his team was totally scared of him.

Dave agreed with the feedback. While Dave wanted his team to like him, he also thought he had plenty of good reason to be angry. He rattled off a list of *situational specifics*: this one person on his team can't quite keep up; that one time a deal almost fell through; the other time the deal did fall through; the day a colleague publicly challenged him in front of his leadership team.

Dave was lost in the leaves.

As we teased it apart, it became clear that Dave's anger—like everyone's—was a defensive emotion shielding him from the more deeply rooted fear of losing control. The question we needed to answer was: What was Dave's anger attempting to protect him from? As we looked more closely across the range of situations that made him angry, Dave realized there was only one common variable: him. To claim his deepest emotional power, he needed to understand what was really triggering a cascade of painful situations in his life. Together, we worked toward the root of it all. His journey to the roots looked like this:

What enraged him so much?

"Mistakes."

What did it mean if somebody made a mistake?

"It means a deal could fall through, or a product launch will fail."

So what?

"It means I've let people down."

And what does that mean?

"It means I've failed."

What do you call someone who fails all the time?

"A loser."

And when a person fundamentally believes he is a loser, what is the emotional energy that the person carries?

"Humiliation."

Beneath the chaos of the leaves and beyond the fury of the trunk, we find the energy that's electrifying the whole system: Dave feared feeling like a humiliated loser.

If you met Dave in real life, you would be stunned that this is his story. On the outside, he was wildly successful, charming, and in charge. He had all the trappings of a happy, successful life. I point this out to you because it's vital you understand all human beings, to varying degrees, carry the energy of humiliation inside of them. Your power move is not to wonder if you have a relationship with humiliation, but to determine what you're doing about it.

When Dave reached the root of his pain—the real energy that was igniting his anger—true transformation was at hand. Dave could stop wasting tremendous energy, wrestling each situation to the ground. Instead, he could focus on a single target: Worthiness.

Turn Humiliation into Worthiness

Pain and power are two sides of the same energetic coin. Within that, humiliation is your root pain and worthiness is your peak power. Your peak emotional power is an unwavering awareness of your own inherent sense of worth—the connection that there's still something energetically good about you *regardless of any situation*. You dramatically expand your edge of emotional power when you fend off your deep fear of humiliation by strengthening your sense of worthiness.

We're so used to being lauded for our *doing* that we automatically assume there's something essential that must be *done* before we can feel worthy. We don't even question it. And we should. If you link your worthiness to *any* activity, you have already lost the plot. If you feel worthier when your coworkers agree with you, when your kids listen to you, or when your partner affirms you, then on the occasions other people won't do it as you want, you are on shaky emotional ground.

I understand that extracting the energy of your worth from the outcomes of your situations seems tough. But a big part of the reason our sense of worth can feel so shaky is because we don't engage ourselves in meaningful reflections about who we are and how we matter outside of the things we do! How are we going to change things we don't even consciously consider?

With that, here are two steps—steps that, on their face, may seem simple—that can actually have a profound effect on engineering an enduring sense of emotional power—of worthiness, self-trust, and self-confidence. They are:

- Releasing them

- Choosing you

Releasing them

Let go of other people's ability to activate *your* energy. Two of the boldest, most straightforward moves you can do to release other people's power over your nervous system are *quit lying* and *stop gossiping*. The only reason we lie or gossip is because we don't believe we're OK as we are.

Let's start with "quit lying." Again, I'm not much for semantics so I don't care if you call it exaggerating, embellishing, playing with the truth, or being inauthentic. The only reason a person chooses to alter the truth of their life is because they think the authentic version of who they are is unacceptable. Lying is so dangerous to your emotional power—to your sense of worth—because it is a deep form of self-rejection. In other words, when you exaggerate things about your life, you inherently reject the "is-ness" of your life. You signal to yourself that the truth of your life is unacceptable *as it is*, that there is something about your life worth betraying. In these moments, you abandon yourself, and when you do, you show yourself that the most dangerous person in the room is you.

It's similar with gossip. We frequently gossip (or vent) about people instead of talking directly to them because we don't feel powerful enough to bring our grievances directly to them. We might feel embarrassed, anxious, or afraid to talk about it. In any case, it signals a weak spot in our emotional power that needs strengthening.

For example, Dave noticed that while he had no problem being gruff with the people who reported to him, he had a lot of trouble talking to peers about his grievances. He had one coworker he found too demanding and unpredictable. When this coworker did something that upset him, Dave would not address it directly. Instead, he would vent to others, "Can you believe what this guy did?" or he would go home and tell his spouse, "Get a load of what he did this time!" For Dave, this form of gossiping—or venting—felt cathartic. But the problem with catharsis is it does not make you emotionally stronger.

The function of gossip is to equalize energy. This is what people mean when they say, "I got that off my chest." When you feel like you've been aggrieved, this creates painful pressure inside of you. For example, if you think someone treated you unfairly, this creates painful feelings of injustice inside of you. Research in both human *and* animal studies shows that injustice agitates the nervous system.[3] When you've been agitated, there is an activation of painful energy inside your nervous system. When you vent or gossip, it's like releasing a pressure valve. The energy of your pain *temporarily* dissipates, but you have done nothing to strengthen your emotional system. This is why gossiping and venting are chronic behaviors; they don't do anything to strengthen your underlying emotional system. When you stop gossiping or venting, you will shift your emotional patterns, which will provoke new insights into how your emotional energy moves and how you now want to choose to engineer your life going forward.

Choosing you

The more we release strategies of inauthenticity, namely lying and gossiping, the closer we come to the truth of our energy. Choosing the authenticity of your own life requires deep attunement with your inner energy—with your inner authority. To do this, grab a journal and a quiet space. Get yourself a room-temperature glass of water, an herbal tea, or whatever beverage calms you. Take ten deep breaths to really calm your nervous system. Then write answers to the following questions. Do not overthink or edit yourself. Just write freely.

Exercise: Releasing Them and Choosing You

Reflect on these questions about self-choosing:

- Would you rather have other people like you, or would you rather like yourself?

- Are you powerful enough to be misunderstood? In other words, when you know something to be true will you adhere to it even if other people don't understand? When you get excited about one of your ideas, do you retain your belief that your idea is excellent even if other people don't agree? Or do you only know the truth of your life based on the reactions of other people?

- Would you rather be interested in your work, or would you rather have other people interested in your work?

- What are the activities you do largely to receive the attention of others? Are there activities in your life you would you stop doing if you knew you would not get external feedback? If so, what are they? (Consider the ways you work, people you engage with, conversations you have, and ways you take care of your body, etc.)

- What are the things about you that would embarrass or humiliate you if other people knew? Why? This may represent an energetic block inside of you. It turns out we are often as sick as our secrets. Are there ways to release this trapped energy that feel safe to you (e.g., talk to a trusted friend, spiritual advisor, mental health professional; create a mini ceremony where you write a letter to "release" this energy and then destroy the letter)?

If you deeply reflected on these questions, you will illuminate a new level of self-awareness. The foundational step to any type of psychological change is always awareness. You may be asking: OK, but what do I *do* with this powerful awareness? Simply select a target and do it. For example, if while reflecting on these questions, you realized you frequently devote more energy to other people's preferences than your own, select a target behavior that would convince you you're releasing the hold that others have over you and starting to more powerfully choose yourself. You could choose any activity. Some examples include:

- Making a bold decision without getting any input from others

- Posting something you like on social media and then turning off comments and notifications so you get no external feedback about what others think

- Practicing sharing your authentic thoughts on a specific topic that you've historically avoided because you feared you would be misunderstood

The specific activity you choose does not matter because it's not the outcome you're after; it's the energy. Seeking your emotional power—your inherent sense of worthiness—from situational outcomes is a lot like frantically looking for your keys when you're already holding them in your hands. When you finally realize the thing you keep looking for "out there" has been with you all along, you access the only thing you wanted anyway: the truth of your own life.

Code 4:
Master Uncertainty

How to stay emotionally powerful
in the energy of uncertainty

t was early in my career when a patient of mine, Jerry, said to me, "I never knew for sure when my dad was gonna beat the shit out of me, so I'd provoke him in the morning. Better to get it out of the way."

This was an early exposure to what I now understand to be one of the most powerful forces in our lives: uncertainty. Uncertainty is life's promise to us all. For more than twenty years, I have watched people rise from unspeakable pain to venture again into a future that withholds all certainty. I work with people who have endured shocking traumas and, predictably, our early conversations are filled with interrogative pleas for a certain safety: "How can I be absolutely sure nothing like this will ever happen again?" they ask me.

The answer is: they cannot.

After many years, the thing that still takes my breath away is the grace and courage of people who accept this truth and say: I rise again not because I know for sure, but because I hope anyway.

The pain of uncertainty is a well-studied neuropsychological phenomenon. For example, when researchers hook people up to machines that deliver electric shocks, people report that it's more painful to be uncertain *if* they may be shocked than it is to be certain they *will* be shocked.[1] This tells you something important: your emotional feelings surrounding your situations of uncertainty can be, quite literally, more painful than physical pain.

Because uncertainty can be so painful, your brain spends a lot of time trying—you guessed it—to avoid it. But like most things with your pain, it is transforming your relationship with this energy that will empower you. A major shift begins when you understand that uncertainty cannot be powerfully understood at the level of the situation. One of the central messages I'm conveying to you across the codes is that if you try to engineer your life on a situation-by-situation basis, you will thwart your emotional evolution. Attempts to reduce uncertainty in every situation it pops up sap your energy because you don't understand the deeper dynamics generating emotional pain across situations.

This neuroenergetic code will show you that uncertainty has a predictable rhythm to its energy, a way it reliably makes you think and feel *regardless of situation.* You become much more emotionally powerful when you take your focus off solving every unresolved scenario and instead focus more on the person you *routinely* become in the shadow of uncertainty's energy.

In this code, we're not trying to avoid uncertainty—because we can't. Instead, we're learning to work with it. This is a critically important distinction because, paradoxically enough, it's the things you do to avoid uncertainty—and not the uncertainty itself—that cause most of your emotional pain.

Earlier we talked about the "overs"—overthinking, overworking, overdoing, and so on. Recall that "overs" are a pain-avoidance response. You might work because you enjoy it, but you *over*work because you are afraid of what *might* happen if you don't. The act of thinking likely brings you plenty of pleasure, but *over*thinking is brutal. And where giving is enjoyable, *over*giving is depleting.

The "overs" are all a defense against anxiety. The logic goes: if I work more, give more, and think more, then I'll be safe. All forms of anxiety—from the mild to the pathological—can be understood as a *dysfunctional relationship with certainty.*[2]

To rise powerfully in the face of a life that promises absolutely no certainty, it helps to first realize how the energy of uncertainty universally behaves. Let me give you a clinical example to make this clear and then I'll apply it to your own life. Take PTSD. PTSD cannot be diagnosed while people are in the throes of active trauma, like combat. You can't diagnose PTSD in the middle of a war zone because the responses that make PTSD *pathological* in a non-traumatic environment are *extremely adaptive* in the midst of trauma. Things like hypervigilance, feeling constantly on guard, or being unable to sleep may save your life if you're in a war.

It's when people return home to safe environments but the safety-seeking behaviors persist that the pathology sets in. For instance, I've worked with combat veterans who refuse to drive cars, ride public transportation, eat at restaurants, shop in stores, or travel to crowded places like hotels or movie theaters because it feels like it *could* be dangerous. The (often unconscious) strategy is to stay safe by avoiding things that are uncertain. In other words, the avoidance of these places is a safety-seeking behavior. The problem, however, is it's not the trauma that's sustaining their pathological anxiety; *it's the safety seeking.* PTSD is not about dangerous things being dangerous; it's about an inability to see safe things as safe.[3]

In your own life, the things you're doing to keep yourself safe from pain—the overdoing, overworking, overgiving, overcommitting—are major causes of your pain. Extreme safety seeking is core to every painful form of anxiety: PTSD, social anxiety, generalized anxiety, OCD. The point here is relevant regardless of whether you have clinically significant anxiety or not. There comes a point when the behaviors you're employing to keep you safe from uncertainty become the very behaviors that injure you.

While the cases in your own life might be less extreme than PTSD, the energy is moving in the same way. For example, you aren't sure if people really like you, so you overdo it around them, trying to become some version of who you believe they think you should be. And then you wonder why you find being around people so depleting. You aren't sure if your social media followers care about you and your content enough, so you overproduce, creating content even when you're drained, and then wonder why you feel so exhausted.

At this point in our conversation, you should see how the energy of uncertainty is at the root of all your forms of anxiety. But there's more. The energy of uncertainty moves through your nervous system in nearly identical ways regardless of the situation that created it. It acts on your brain and body in predictable ways. Neurophysiological studies show that even minor forms of uncertainty produce changes to physiology, including brain activations in regions involved in threat detection and decision-making as well as increased sweating.[4] Do some situations make your thoughts race more or your heart pound harder? Absolutely, but this is a difference in degree, not type. In other words, the energy of uncertainty affects your nervous system in similar ways across a range of diverse situations.

You take back your power when you realize that—as with humiliation—the energy of uncertainty does not live *in* the situation but is *itself the energy that creates the situation.* Your situation doesn't make you wonder "What if?" Rather, it's the act of anxiously wondering "What if?" that shapes your situation.

To work with uncertainty's energy in a way that empowers your leadership, be the hero of your own story.

Exercise: Be the Hero of Your Own Story

Although you are not the most powerful person in life, you are absolutely the most powerful person in *your own* life. While it is true that you cannot be certain if the sun will rise tomorrow or if a meteor will fall on your house tonight, nearly all the pain uncertainty provokes in your life comes not from bizarre acts of nature but from your fears about other people's behavior:

- What if you do what you want to do and people get mad at you?

- What if you say what you want to say and people misunderstand you?

- What if these people don't like your idea?

- What if those people don't agree with you?

- What if your kids don't listen to you?

- What if your spouse won't support you?

When you manage this uncertainty by trying to be something you don't even want to be, pain is your inevitable consequence. Examples include:

- You keep your mouth shut when you want to speak up.

- You have bold ideas inside of you, but you play small for other people.

- You say yes when you mean no.

- You work when your body is pleading for rest.

Recall our definition of pain: It's self-division, the times you abandon yourself by dividing yourself from yourself.

When you try to overcontrol every uncertain contingency, you lose the plot of your own story. Worst of all, you spend all your energy playing the part in a life you don't even want anyway. The "overs" you're doing to manage your uncertainty are intended to keep you safe. But how good is "safe" if it ultimately means you're exhausted, repressed, self-rejecting, and unfulfilled?

To change the way you feel, become your own source of safety—be the hero of your own story. Here's how:

- Be an information seeker, not a reassurance seeker.

- Say "I don't know."

Be an information seeker, not a reassurance seeker

Now that you understand that so much of your anxiety, stress, and worry are caused by a dysfunctional relationship with certainty, you need to know another paradox. If you regularly find yourself feeling anxious, there's probably one thing you're doing to relieve your anxiety that's making it worse: seeking reassurance.

Reassurance-seeking behavior, as its name suggests, occurs when you look to other people for guarantees about certainty that they cannot actually provide. Reassurance seeking is the act of looking for certain answers to unanswerable questions. While reassurance seeking may make you feel better in the moment, it weakens your emotional power over time.

Reassurance seeking is different from information seeking. Where information seeking intends to answer a question, reassurance seeking is aimed at creating certainty. Reassurance seeking happens at the level of emotion; for example, "How would you feel if he talked to you like that?" Information seeking happens at the level of fact; for example, "What's the most evidence-based treatment for anxiety?"

Have you ever:

- Asked another person if they would have done the same thing you did?

- Asked one person for their opinion on a situation, have it not resolve your anxiety, and then continued asking until you found someone who gave you the answer you wanted?

- Asked for technical advice from someone who had no expertise in this area? For example, maybe you were worried about your child's behavior and so you asked someone with no formal expertise, "This seems normal to you, right?"

These are all reassurance-seeking behaviors that, when done chronically, *insidiously* weaken your emotional power. When you get the reassurance you were seeking, you experience a temporary bump in your sense of control. Suddenly, you feel calmed because the person's answer gave you the temporary illusion of certainty. But here's the catch: when you restore your sense of emotional safety using an external source, you further destabilize your safety because *you* then believe that the thing you need to regulate your nervous system isn't your own inner authority, but someone else's opinion. This then creates the sense that you're not the hero in your own story; someone else is.

Of course, it's healthy to seek other people's advice from time to time. We're not meant to live or lead in a vacuum. However, there's a vast difference between occasionally seeking to bounce ideas off someone versus needing other people's opinions to hold your own emotional posture upright.

Remember: reassurance is not information. Asking a financial advisor for their expert opinion on finances is different than asking your mom, your spouse, and someone on social media what they would have done if the customer spoke to them like that.

There are beautiful words to describe leadership. One of those words is "self-assured," which literally means to be able to be assured by your *self*. To be a powerful leader, you'll need to strengthen your ability to be your own hero—to be the surest source of your own reassurance.

To determine where you might want to become more information seeking and less reassurance seeking, here's an exercise. Review the list in table 2 and note the items that tend to describe your behavior. Reflect on your answers and decide where you might want to start exhibiting more information-seeking behaviors and fewer reassurance-seeking ones.

Say "I don't know"

In the face of uncertainty, it takes a very powerful person to admit the truth and say, "I don't know." As a leader, there can be pressure on you to produce answers you do not yet have. Whether you're

TABLE 2

Information seeking and reassurance seeking

Information seeker	Reassurance seeker
Asks questions to learn	Asks questions to be relieved
Open to all responses	Needs specific answer
Asks question once	Asks question repeatedly
Asks qualified people	Asks unqualified people
Asks answerable questions	Asks unanswerable questions
Accepts answer even if it's undesirable	Responds to undesirable answer by challenging it, insisting the answer be rephrased, or finding someone else to provide desired answer
Can handle ambiguity	Demands certainty
Seeks answer for clear purpose	Perpetually seeking "information" but cannot reach confident conclusion

Source: Adapted from worksheet from the Anxiety Disorders Center, St. Louis Behavioral Medicine Institute, https://iocdf.org/wp-content/uploads/2016/04/18-Information-seekers-vs-reassurance-seekers.pdf.

leading a business, a household, a conversation, or your children, you're used to people looking to you when they feel uncertain. Under this pressure, there can be a natural reflex to try to deliver what you think they're expecting from you.

When you are uncertain, you only have two choices: you can pretend to know, or you can tell the truth. If you want to be the hero of your own story, you have to be empowered to say three brave words: *I. Don't. Know.*

Pretending to know something you don't is an insidious form of people-pleasing. One senior leader said to me, "I always feel pressure to give people answers to questions I don't have. I don't want them to be disappointed, and so I frequently give answers or make promises that cause me headaches later on."

In this leader's case, it was challenging for him to say "I don't know" because he thought *his safety* depended on *their certainty*. Because he could not bear the pain of other people's disappointment, he told them what they wanted to hear. If you're afraid people will be disappointed in you or reject your leadership if you don't have answers, you'll be tempted to people-please by giving them the certainty you think they're asking for. The problem is that while a certain answer may make sense in their story, it doesn't make sense in yours.

Do you want to be the hero in their story or in yours?

There's a fine but powerful balance between a false certainty and an honest clarity. During the wildly uncertain times of 2020, I was working with two different organizations. Everyone was frantically trying to figure out what was happening with everything.

In one of the organizations, the leadership sat behind closed doors and communicated virtually nothing to their staff. The tragic irony is that these leaders genuinely cared about their staff's well-being; they just weren't communicating it effectively. They were stalling because they believed that they needed to have certain answers to things no one yet knew, like what would happen with Covid-19, what the work policies would be, if there would be layoffs, and when this would all happen. Although I urged them to tell their staff the truth, they continuously said the optics didn't look strong for a leadership team not to have answers. But their decision to wait for some illusory perfect knowingness wasn't a sign of leadership power; it was a sign of fear. And under this wobbly energy, employee engagement scores plummeted.

The other organization was grappling with similar uncertainty, but they communicated this clearly and regularly to their staff. For example, the CEO would regularly hold virtual meetings with her staff, saying things like "We still don't know the answer to many questions, but we're committed to answering them, and I'll be meeting with you again in three days to give you another update—*even if it's just to say, 'I still don't know.'*" She pledged to be transparent and honest with her staff, and her staff loved it. In fact, she was surprised to see—at a time when the world was in turmoil—her organization's employee engagement scores stayed steady. She said to me, "Who knew that telling people I didn't have answers would be the smart-est thing I could do?"

Something big starts to happen when you begin to boldly own the power of your "I don't know." As with the case of the CEO above, you start to clearly see evidence that all the bad things you were terrified would happen if you said, "I don't know" don't materialize. When you as the leader send a clear signal to your team, your children, or your partner that they can live honestly with you, you create relationships rooted in emotional freedom—and emotionally free people are the most powerful people in the world.

. . .

Response to uncertainty is, as you will see in the next chapter, a learned behavior you acquired during your childhood. The problem this poses for the way you lead your life today is that the strategies that served you as a child are often the ones that often diminish your influence today.

When times are uncertain, the people who depend on you—whether it's your team, your customers, or your kids—are looking to you. Uncertain times definitionally mean the external environment no longer provides a clear answer. This means *you* are the answer. You are the one your people are waiting for. Your old relationship with uncertainty, a relationship based on adaptive but ultimately ill-fitting childhood patterning, has already taken you to the edge of what it can deliver. A new relationship is coming.

Answer the call.

Code 5: Rewire Your Source Code

How childhood connects to the way you lead your life and what to do about it

This neuroenergetic code takes you to the origins of your emotional power—to the earliest ways you learned to lead yourself through tough situations at work, at home, and in relationships. To get there, let's start with a question: Who first taught you about leading yourself and others?

Your parents.

To strengthen the way you lead, this code is dedicated to examining your parents as the most powerful leaders in your life. Note that I did not say the most loving leaders. Nor the most attentive, helpful, smart, or even the most present. I hope your parents were all those things. But the inescapable fact is that *whatever* your parents did—the good, the bad, and the in-between—it was *the most powerful* because of what was happening in your brain at the time they were doing it.

Converging evidence across a range of scientific disciplines from clinical psychology to neuroscience to developmental psychology demonstrates the unparalleled power of the parent-child relationship.[1] During the first three years of your life, your brain underwent spectacular development, producing more than a million neural connections each second.[2] From the moment you were born, your parents were already teaching you what would become your most formative lessons about emotions and relationships.

They were the ones who first taught you about power and pain, about who shows up and who doesn't, about when you matter and when you don't. Their influence—the ways they looked at you, spoke to you, helped you, loved you, and harmed you—created the foundation of your energetic makeup. And it's this foundation that has very much to do with how you lead yourself today.

We'll refer to your early childhood experiences that shaped your development as your "source code" as it represents the source of who you are. The brain development of children is deeply influenced by the quality of the relationship with their parents. Your parents' parenting style had a profound effect on your biology, like the function of your brain and the expression of your genes.[3]

We've talked at length about how your brain is a pattern-detection machine electrified by emotional energies. The most powerful patterns of your life are the ones erected during your childhood. It is our earliest pattern that becomes our most enduring. Oddly, however, although your earliest life experiences inexorably inform your adult life, you cannot consciously access many of them. Subsequently, it's easy to think that ancient events you can barely recall can't be *that* relevant to your present-day leadership.

But they are.

It's not that your brain doesn't remember; it does. It's just that your child brain had not yet developed the regions necessary to translate things that happened into stories you recall. The way your brain retains memories is spectacular and multifaceted. It stores memories of events like birthday parties differently than facts like capital cities. It's different again for how it stores memories for procedures like brushing your teeth, and different still for memories of spatial awareness like remembering a route to a familiar place.[4] Neuroscientific evidence shows that you encode memories far beyond what you're able to consciously access through words.[5]

Research also suggests you routinely began to hold conscious memory around age seven.[6] But—get this—it's your years *before* you turned seven that are most powerful for your brain's development. Your source code, the original patterning of who you would ultimately grow up to be, was constructed at a time you can't fully access. It is profoundly terrifying and awe-inspiring to realize that you are not the originator of your deepest story, but rather an actor in it. (If there's a stronger argument for our stunning interdependence, I cannot think of one.)

The strategies you developed as a child were brilliant for leading you through childhood, but they tend to lose their effectiveness as time goes on. If your father was a dangerous man, for example, pleasing him would have been adaptive for you as a young child. But to carry this "coding" into your adult life, where you now please all people with power—well, that's no longer so adaptive. Strategies that worked brilliantly for us at seven hinder us at forty-seven.

Research from a range of fields, including industrial organizational psychology and clinical psychology, demonstrates that quality of our relationship with our parents affects the ways we lead ourselves at work, as parents, and as partners.[7] In the realm of work, for example, studies show that individuals who experienced their parents as comforting and responsive are more likely to be transformational leaders.

The purpose of rewiring your source code is to improve internalized—and often unconscious—childhood coding that is currently blocking the full expression of your emotional power. We will do this through a four-step exercise. Each step builds on the one before it:

1. **Remember:** First, you will remember your source code by answering a series of questions designed to bring unconscious material into your conscious awareness so it can be worked on.

2. **Relate:** Once you remember your source code, relate it to your life. No matter what happened to you, if it's not relevant to your life today, who cares?

3. **Recognize:** Once you've figured out how your source code is related to your present-day life, you will start to recognize how it precisely blocks a more powerful expression of your leadership.

4. **Rewire:** Finally, you will rewire your source code by choosing your clear and empowering alternatives.

I realize you may have had several formative leaders in your life. However, I strongly encourage you to focus on your earliest caretakers to get the most impact from these exercises. Whoever oversaw most of your care from birth to age five will have built the energetic foundation from which you now live and lead. This could be your biological parents, adoptive parents, grandparents, or an older sibling. For most of us, our earliest caretakers were our mother and our father. Note that even if one or both of your parents were absent, this absence creates powerful energetic effects that shape the entire course of your life. In other words, whether our parents were always there or never there, that fact invariably shapes us for better and for worse.

Exercise: The Four Steps to Rewire Your Source Code

Rewiring your source code is essential to accessing a more mature expression of your emotional power. The steps in this process will guide you in strengthening your source code.

Step 1: Remember your source code

To free yourself from constrictive childhood conditioning is to achieve the freedom to lead, not as you were programmed, but as you choose. This exercise will help you answer the question: What did it feel like back then? Before you can change patterns that hamstring your power today, you must consciously access the source of those patterns. As we discussed, much of the patterning you received in early childhood is contained in unconscious memory stores in your brain. It's when you work to bring old coding into conscious awareness that you can change your patterns. To access the root of your source code, reflect on the following.

YOUR PARENTS AND YOUR POWER. For a child, positive parental attention is the most powerful energy on the planet. What patterns generally worked to capture the power of your parents' positive attention? Here are some examples. Customize an answer that fits your experience best.

To get my parents' positive attention, I often felt like I had to:

- be right

- be very successful or win (e.g., at sports, academics, arguments)

- make no mistakes

- act socially acceptable (e.g., be polite)

- do what other people want

- be attractive

- be athletic

- be thin

- be quiet

- be very responsible

- be strong

- fix other people's mood

- take care of people

- take care of chores

- achieve a lot

- be nonemotional or hyperrational

- be fun because that's the only time the fighting would stop

- create your own: _____

YOUR PARENTS AND YOUR PAIN. Your parents, in their humanity, invariably caused you pain. What were some of the common ways that your parents caused you pain? Here are some examples. Customize an answer that fits your experience best.

My parents hurt me when they:

- ignored me

- criticized or shamed me

- depended on me too much

- compared me to others

- showed me too many of their emotions

- yelled at me or others

- physically abused me or others

- verbally insulted me or others

- told me that I was being unreasonable and/or selfish

- idealized me

- made me feel like I was their savior

- made me feel like their life's dreams depended on me

- were overbearing

- relied on me too much for support around the house (e.g., with little siblings; with chores; with their problems)

- create your own: _____

YOUR PARENTS AND THEIR PAIN. How did you witness your parents relate to their own pain? In other words, what did your parents teach you as you watched them handle their own stress, frustration, exhaustion, sadness, disappointment, and other painful emotions? Here are some examples. Customize an answer that fits your experience best.

Did they:

- calmly acknowledge they were feeling upset

- gently ask for an appropriate amount of time to themselves

- engage in self-care

- share their pain in ways that were developmentally appropriate for the parent-child relationship (e.g., "Mommy's feeling sad right now, but sadness is normal. You don't have to worry.")

- become short, terse, or rude

- control others

- behave in frightening or violent ways

- use substances or other addictive behaviors (e.g., gambling)

- withdraw or withhold (e.g., give the silent treatment; leave the house for extended periods of time; lock themselves in their bedroom)

- overwork

- become passive-aggressive

- yell or cry

- throw temper tantrums

- behave in self-defeating ways (e.g., comments like: "Nothing ever works out for me" or behaviors like quitting jobs or canceling events at the last minute)

- become hypercritical of other people's work

- blame others

- numb their pain

- hide their pain

- create your own: _____

Your answers here are intended to help you remember your source code. Review all your answers from the lists above and then create a summary of what you've remembered. By creating a cogent summary, you're remembering early patterns you learned about pain so that you can more consciously understand how old "coding" is affecting your present-day leadership. Including brief examples of specific memories where your parents taught you about pain can be very powerful as you work to draw old memories into greater conscious awareness. This summary is deeply personal; you can write it any way you want. When you're satisfied with your summary, keep it close. We'll build on it more in the next step.

Here's an example from Noah, a brilliant software engineer:

> To get my parents' positive attention, I had to—oddly enough—not need much of their attention. My dad put a huge premium on independence. I now realize it didn't feel like freedom; it felt like neglect. When I was six years old, my dad told me I had to earn money to pay for my own birthday party. I was six! When I was 15, my dad used to tell me to drive to the store for him. When I mentioned it was illegal for 15-year-olds to drive alone and that I was afraid of being stopped by the police, my dad told me to "drive like a man and then I wouldn't have to worry about the police." Once, I got pulled over and taken down to the station. It took my dad hours to come get me. When I asked him why he left me for so long, he said it was to teach me a lesson for making stupid decisions. It was crazymaking. My dad taught me it was dangerous to

depend on anyone but myself. My mom hurt me in her passivity—she was awesome, but too eager to keep the peace with my dad so she never defended me when he was harsh or neglectful.

Step 2: Recover the relevance of the source code

Now that you've identified energies of your childhood pain—either ones you experienced directly from your parents or ones you witnessed in your parents—you can link these early life lessons to how you lead today.

Note that the energy of your childhood patterning tends to present itself as either a *because of* energy or an *in spite of* energy. For example, "I felt consistently criticized by my mother and today I'm critical of my team" is an example of *because of* energy. Whereas if you do the inverse of what was done to you, that's *in spite of* energy. For example, "My dad was very volatile. I saw him lose jobs and struggle to find work. Today, I am extremely reliable—so reliable that I can be rigid and unrelenting."

Here are a few examples of how this early childhood coding may be energizing your leadership today:

- If you were consistently dodging your parents' explosive moods, you may behave in inconsistent, unreliable, or irresponsible ways today.

- If you consistently felt like you had to be the best, you may behave in aggressive or hypercompetitive ways today, or you may find yourself unable to tolerate even minor losses.

- If you consistently felt neglected by your parents, you may have difficulty connecting with people today.

- If you consistently felt judged by your parents, you may have difficulty feeling good enough today.

- If you consistently felt unseen as a child, you may find you never feel sufficiently recognized today.

- If you consistently felt controlled by your parents, you may be so independent that you are difficult to work with today.

- Create your own: _____

Note, too, if there are any patterns you realize apply with men, but not with women—or vice versa. It's not uncommon for people to have different reactions to men and women. For example, I worked with a CHRO, Eli, who was not intimidated by men. His boss, the CEO of a large international company, was a man, and Eli was comfortable around him. However, Eli was intimidated by and very people-pleasing toward women, including junior colleagues. Eli was very frightened by his mother but felt safe with his father.

With all this in mind, return to your summary. Building off what you wrote, add how you see the relevance of your source code affecting you today. This part of your summary should identify something you have been wanting in your life but haven't yet been able to achieve. It could be anything—a promotion, growing your business, feeling more respected by your kids, or being understood by your partner. The relevance section of your summary answers the question "What about my childhood experiences remind me of what I don't have in my life today?" Don't overthink it or judge it. Simply write.

In Noah's case, he had been wanting to manage a bigger team but had been denied multiple opportunities. Let's return to his example:

> For a while I've wanted to manage more people at work, but I keep getting feedback at my performance evaluations that I need to understand how to work more effectively with people—how to both rely on people more and show people they can rely on me. After remembering my source code, I see that my family ethos was "every person for themselves." As a kid, I had way too much freedom and had to figure out basically everything for myself. What I didn't learn to do was ask

for help and, because I wasn't allowed to ask for help from my parents, I didn't learn how to give help to other people. In fact, I've heard in my 360s that people are afraid to ask me for things because they say I look "annoyed" and that I ignore people who aren't high performers. But the truth is, I'm overwhelmed. I don't know how to help them. I feel bad I can't help them, and I worry that their inability to figure it out will derail me, too. This source code has helped me so much because I've been banging my head against the wall trying to advance my career and start managing more people. I now know precisely where I've been stuck and what to work on.

Step 3: Recognize your source code

Once you're clear on the general relevance of your childhood programming to your present-day life, you're ready to determine what *specific* behaviors your source code causes that are weakening the way you lead in your career and in your home.

Whenever your childhood source code gets triggered and you act upon it, you cannot *respond* from the unfiltered power of your emotional presence. You're *reacting* from old childhood patterning. There's a big difference between being mad and being trigger mad. If you get rudely cut off at a stop sign and you're upset about it for the next two miles, that's mad. But if you're still talking about it next week, that's trigger mad. When you *overreact* to a comment from your spouse or a conversation with a coworker, it is because your source code has been triggered. However, until you recognize that a major component of what triggered you is ancient energy and not real-time interaction, you will stay stuck at the level of the trigger.

In my work with Nina, a high-performing leader and mother of three young children, we spent considerable time examining her source code. Nina's primary pain point was that she overreacted to things—she got too hot, too quickly, too often. One day, her husband ate the last pickle and put the empty jar back in the refrigerator. When she saw it, she described being hit with a "hot flash of rage." She grabbed the empty jar and started screaming, "Why does everyone in my life exploit me?!" Suddenly, she burst into laughter. "There was just something so absurd about me screaming bloody murder about exploitation and pickles. In that moment, I understood that so much of my behavior had nothing to do with what I thought it had to do with. Pickles saved my family."

When your source code gets triggered, your nervous system will respond in one of five defensive ways. While most people have heard about the fight-or-flight response, there are three additional nervous system activations that may resonate with you: freeze, fawn, and fall apart. After reviewing each of the five defensive responses below, decide how your nervous system most commonly responds when you're triggered. Notice, too, if your nervous system responds in different ways in different environments (e.g., home vs. work) or with different people (e.g., your kids vs. your boss).

FIGHT. Fight occurs when you get activated and you get aggressive. This response might look like:

- combative language

- condescending language

- shouting

- stomping

- hitting

- slamming a fist on a table

- being aggressive with property (e.g., tearing paper, tossing a pen, slamming a door)

- blocking exits

- aggressively interrupting

- short, terse language

- intimidating body language

- rude gestures, like eye rolls or sighs

Example: Recall Dave, the senior leader of a large tech company, who learned that his situational anger was just masking his energy of humiliation. Before he transformed his energy, Dave spent a lot of time being angry. When his nervous system got activated, he would often speak threateningly to his staff, saying things like, "I don't care what you have to do to get it done; you better get it done."

FLIGHT. Flight occurs when you get activated and you tend to get away as fast as you can. This response might look like:

- avoiding people who trigger you

- being busy with household chores so you don't have to talk to your partner

- refusing to ask for help even when you need it because you feel too scared

- coming into meetings/social functions too late or leaving too early as a way of avoiding social interactions

- putting the TV on for your kids so you don't have to engage with them

- focusing on your smartphone to avoid interacting with people

- attributing your desires to other people because you're too scared to say what you want

- making excuses for why you can't be present for certain things

Example: When Alex, a marketing and communications leader, got triggered around certain colleagues, it became difficult for her to hold her own opinions because she was afraid of people's reactions. So, if she wanted to take a project in a new direction, she would tell certain colleagues that the change was other people's idea, rather than claiming ownership of something she wanted to do.

FREEZE. Freeze occurs when you get activated and are unable to fight or run from a threat. Freeze is reactive immobility. Unlike fight and flight responses that "speed up" your nervous system, the freeze response slows it down and puts you in a depressed or hypoaroused state. Your heart rate accelerates with fight or flight; it decelerates with freeze.[8]

The freeze response occurs when our brains decide we cannot directly confront the threat and are unable to escape. Upon threat, both sympathetic and parasympathetic branches of the autonomic nervous system activate. However, while the fight-or-flight response is controlled by sympathetic activity, the freeze response is dominated by parasympathetic activity.[9] For example, an antelope that hears a lion may try to neither fight the lion nor run from the lion and instead freeze to avoid detection.

In your life, this might look like:

feeling too overwhelmed to do anything

feeling a sudden drop in your energy (e.g., being upbeat and suddenly down)

feeling a sudden onset of fatigue

being unable to speak

being unable to move

feeling paralyzed; unable to do anything

feeling numb

feeling apathetic or uninspired

shutting down

changes in your voice

feeling foggy, lethargic, or disconnected

Example: Shanice, a senior client manager at a global consulting firm, described her emotional state during the 2020 lockdown: "I am a high-energy, extroverted busybody. These days, I barely recognize myself. I should feel something, but it's like I don't even have the energy to feel my feelings. I'm just low. Not sad, but low: low energy, low mood, low voice, low everything. I feel paralyzed by everything."

FAWN. Fawn occurs when you get activated and try to people-please not because you *want* to but because you feel like you *have* to in order to stay safe. Research understands this form of appeasement—or people-pleasing—as a survival response to perceived entrapment.[10]

This might look like repeatedly:

saying yes when you want to say no	acting like it's your job to fix other people's bad mood
offering flattery or compliments to others as a form of reducing your own anxiety	engaging in activities you don't want to do just to appease others
constantly checking if people like you	only feeling OK if you know others are OK
apologizing even when it's unnecessary	needing other people to agree with you before you feel confident
asking if people are mad at you	asking other people for their permission for things you don't need their permission to do

Example: Matt, the director at an e-commerce company, was often obsequious in communications with certain colleagues and clients. A colleague mentioned a minor error made by Matt's team. Matt said he could not stop thinking about it, wondering if the colleague thought he was an incompetent leader. He ended up sending him an excessively accommodating email, saying: "I'm so deeply sorry for the inconvenience. We will 100 percent make sure this doesn't happen again." Importantly, Matt did not *want* to send this email, but felt he *needed* to.

FALL APART. This is the energy you activate if something relatively minor goes wrong and you interpret it as a disaster. This might look like:

a tendency to speak in catastrophic language: "The whole thing is ruined!" or "This can never be fixed"	ruminating about potential worst-case scenarios (e.g., "If I don't nail this presentation, my whole career is over")
seeing small errors as major problems (e.g., "If there's a typo in the email, then people will think I'm incompetent")	difficulty recovering or proceeding when something doesn't go according to plan

believing a relationship is ruined if someone disappoints you

thinking in black-or-white terms (e.g., thinking you are always wrong or someone else is always right)

requiring perfectionism as a threshold for safety (e.g., "Everyone must like my idea or it's terrible")

refusing to engage with others after discord until they "fix it"

Example: Adriana was an industry leader in human resources. Given her expertise, she was asked to be the keynote speaker at a large virtual event. During the conference, her internet connection experienced a one-minute glitch where her screen froze. Quickly, her connection was restored and the rest of her speech was flawless. Although she received glowing feedback from the audience, who completed an online survey about her speech, Adriana insisted that her talk had been a "total disaster."

Step 4: Rewire your source code

Now that you understand how your source code shows up and what you've been reflexively doing when it's activated, it's time to rewire it in a way that empowers you. On a sheet of paper, draw two columns. On the top left, write "Pain caused by my source code." On the top right, write "Rewiring my source code." (See table 3.)

Under "Pain caused by my source code," list everything you learned from this exercise about how you may lead yourself in ways you do not like. For this exercise to have maximum effect, be specific about what you're doing that you don't like and link it to your childhood. For example, don't write, "I'm too apologetic." Instead write, "I say sorry all the time to my male colleagues. It reminds me of how I used to apologize to my dad to keep him from blowing up." Don't write, "Sometimes I'm critical." Instead write, "When my partner tries to get the kids to school, I get critical, telling them they shouldn't rush the kids so much in the morning because it's bad parenting. It reminds me of how my mother was always telling me a better way to do it."

Describe specific people and situations. This is deeply personal to you, and you can be as private as you choose. There's no right or wrong way. Simply write down anything you hope to "rewire." Below are some more examples to help you calibrate:

- Lon, who is slightly senior to me in our organization, intimidates me and I flee. I try to avoid all meetings with him and, if I can't, I refuse to speak when I'm around him.

- When Laura doesn't agree with me, I tend to be passive-aggressive by not responding to her emails.

- As an entrepreneur, I don't show up as consistently as I could because I'm constantly afraid of being judged. I was the kid who got a 99 percent on a test, and my dad's first question would be "What question did you get wrong?" Now, I'm spending too much time "getting ready" and not enough time showing up.

- When my kids are upset about something I know is relatively minor, I fall apart, ruminating and asking my partner repeatedly if I'm a terrible parent.

- When people who are junior on my team don't perform as well as I hope, I punish them by ignoring or being less responsive to them.

- I fawn by saying "I'm sorry" too much.

- I compliment people in order to reduce my own anxiety.

In the second column, write down *highly specific alternatives.* Do not leave room for confusion or ambiguity. Describe 1) specific behaviors you will now adopt, 2) more powerful alternative statements you now choose to make, and 3) the precise amount of time you plan to implement these new behaviors. The more you customize this to fit the truth of your own life, the more powerful you can expect the rewiring to be. Table 3 contains a few examples to help you calibrate.

TABLE 3

Your source code

Pain caused by my source code	Rewiring my source code
I fawn by saying "sorry" too much. I used to apologize all the time to my dad to keep him from blowing up.	For one week, I will not apologize to anyone.
Lon intimidates me because he's withholding and critical. I've realized his energy reminds me of my mother. When I'm in a meeting with him, I rarely speak.	No matter what, I will say something in every single interaction I have with Lon for the next month. Even if I simply pass him in the hallway, I will say something. If I happen to freeze and I'm unable to say something relevant, my plan is to specifically make a comment about the weather.
When my kids are upset about something I know is relatively minor, I fall apart, ruminating and asking my partner repeatedly if I'm a terrible parent. This reminds me of my mom, who was always looking for validation.	For two weeks, I will ask for absolutely no reassurance from my partner.

As you review these statements, notice if you think the rewiring exercises are too extreme. For example, maybe you think it's unreasonable to not ask for *any* reassurance from your partner. After all, why bother having a relationship if you can't get support in your moments of need? But, two things: First, note that the rewiring exercises have *very specific time frames*. You're not never again asking for support from your partner; you're avoiding reassurance for a predetermined and reasonable amount of time.

Second, remember that in neuroenergetic code 1 we talked about how there is no escaping all pain—and that the more you try to avoid all pain, the more you actually exacerbate your pain. Code 1 taught you to pick a more powerful pain, a new level of resistance that will ultimately make you stronger. It will be distressing if you deny yourself the reassurance you're accustomed to seeking—and that's precisely the point. To revisit our physical strength analogy, if you want to run an eight-minute mile, you can't keep running ten-minute miles. If, as you're trying to override your source code with more powerful alternatives and you make repeated exceptions—just this once it's *super* vital that you apologize to Mary for forgetting to include her on the email, and also you really were going to speak up but did *everyone not see the expression on Tom's face*—you will not be able to expand your emotional power beyond the edge of what you can currently tolerate.

Know this: Your brain *will* play tricks on you as you work to become more powerful. It *will* freak you out and tell you that you will become a frumpy troll whom the whole world will turn into an ugly meme if you don't immediately—*and. I. do. mean. immediately*—[fill in the blank]. This is just a quick meltdown of the brain and nothing to be alarmed about. Hold your emotional shake and endure the growing pains necessary to rest comfortably in your new level of power.

PART TWO

Connecting to Others

Connecting to Others

Neuroenergetic codes for connecting to others

Before we move on to the next code for strengthening your emotional leadership in relationships, we need to note the shift that's happening in the advice I'm giving you. The first five neuroenergetic codes helped you adjust your own emotional posture. Those five codes offered core lessons to understand how to strengthen your *intrapersonal* power—your ability to lead yourself. Before you can help others, you must first possess the level of emotional intelligence you hope to inspire. Just like you can't teach other people calculus until you yourself know how to do calculus, you can't lead people through emotionally painful times until you know how to deal with your own energy in emotionally painful times.

With part 1 under your belt, you understand how to exponentially increase your own emotional power. Now, we can turn to the three *interpersonal* codes—the leading of others. As we get into these codes, we need to understand that there's one core concept that creates all pain in relationships: difference.

When people come to me because their relationships are in distress either at home or at work, they nearly always begin by describing situations like this:

- This person wants to do this, but I want to do that.

- She thinks we should be more visionary in our approach, but I think we should be more practical.

- He talks to me in that tone, but I want him to talk to me in this one.

- This person wants to spend the money like this, but I want to spend the money like that.

- This person wants to spend our time like this, but I want to spend our time like that.

- These people want to raise the prices, but those people don't.

- These people believe in these rights, but those people don't.

- These people want to invade this country, but those people don't.

There are infinite ways people can be upset, irritated, betrayed, or repulsed by each other. If you don't know how to think in emotionally intelligent ways about interpersonal difference, it's easy to feel pained by it. You position yourself as much more emotionally powerful when you understand that all conflict begins when your brain's threat networks activate in response to difference.

Because we live in a world that does not teach us how to intelligently handle difference, our confusion about difference often leads us to interpret it as dangerous. We feel threatened by the fact that other people want to behave in ways that don't make sense to us. You can intelligently lead people only to the degree that you can manage difference.

Consider for a moment: How many people do you presently lead? How many people report to you? How many people are you in charge of educating? How many children do you have? How many social media followers actively engage with you? How many people in your family depend on your leadership? How many people regularly look for your guidance?

Imagine that you currently run a coaching business and you do group coaching for about twenty people. These twenty people are very happy with your leadership; they deeply appreciate their connection to you and value the content you give them. This means you are an energetic match for those twenty customers.

Now, imagine that you started one day with twenty people enrolled in your program and woke up the next day with two thousand people. Chances are that this exponential growth would be too much for your nervous system to handle. Even if you were initially excited, your mind would likely soon race with painful doubts. Could you handle that many people? How would you develop a connection with all these new customers? Would people feel satisfied by the services you were offering? Sure, you could keep twenty people happy, but complaints are now inevitable with two thousand. How will you react to the criticism?

Beneath the frenzy of all those situational questions is the energetic root that unites all your fears. What you're really upset about is what happens to you if there's more *difference* than your nervous system can handle.

What happens if people are at odds with you—if they're mad at you, dissatisfied with you, or disappointed in you? Even if you say your concerns are more logistical—for instance, worrying that your website can't handle all that traffic—remember there is never any problem unless there's emotional pain. So, you must have some *feeling* about the website going sideways—and it's going to be something like you would *feel* incompetent, humiliated, embarrassed, or anxious because people are wanting something different than what you're presently providing.

Previously, I worked in politics—at the White House, on various presidential campaigns, and for a political consulting firm. One thing my work in politics has shown me is that people can very much believe they can handle the energy of something they are not actually equipped to handle. For example, there were political candidates who swore they could hold the pressure of public office and yet were ultimately unable to handle the pressure of being so intensely in the public eye. The energy of office—the difference between what other people demanded of them and what they wanted for themselves—was too much for their nervous system to hold.

There is no shame holding the energy you are currently conditioned to hold. It just is. Just like you can't run a nine-minute mile if you're only conditioned to run an eleven-minute mile, your nervous system only has the strength to handle what it has been conditioned to handle. It's emotional math. This is why the very first code in this book was devoted to using your pain to expand the amount of energy your nervous system could handle.

Right now, there's a certain number of people you can confidently hold as part of your team, organization, household, or social network before you get too provoked by differences—their different demands, preferences, schedules, and ideas. If you exceed this number before you're ready, your leadership will stumble. You'll be too anxious, too insecure, and too overwhelmed to lead powerfully. Just like there is no optimal mile pace, there is no optimal number of people to hold in your energetic sphere. It simply depends on what your preference is. You get to choose what your leadership looks like.

Regardless of the number of people you lead, chances are good that you want to show up as exceptionally magnetic in your relationships—you want people to *want* to be led by you. You want your team to want to work for you, your customers to want to buy from you, your kids to want to listen to you, and your partner to want to trust you. If so, you must understand that every interpersonal problem comes down to two competing drives of the brain:

- The drive for independence

- The drive for dependence

Independence is just another word for difference. People have a deep drive for freedom—freedom to think differently, work differently, feel differently, and relate differently. Whether you call it independence, difference, choice, preference, autonomy, or freedom, the semantics do not matter because the underlying neurology is about an individual's drive to choose a life that makes the most sense to them.

This drive for independence begins very early in life. When my daughter was not yet two, she developed a very strong—and ever-changing!—preference for the color of her drinking cups. God help you if you happened to give her the orange cup when girlfriend wanted the yellow cup. Or the blue cup. Or the green cup.

Very early in development, she was expressing her drive for difference—her drive for choice. This desire for independence is very strong and can create tremendous pain in our relationships. But the *only* reason the drive for independence ever creates any pain in your relationships is because it's coupled with a competing need: *a need for dependence.*

Here again, it does not matter what word you use: dependence, connection, closeness, friendship, love, attachment, or attunement. The neurobiological necessity for connection is on clear display from the beginning of our lives. The infant's nervous system is largely regulated by its connection to caretakers. Parents' willingness to feed, hold, speak, and generally tend to their babies' needs is a requirement for survival.[1] But this interconnectivity of our nervous systems does not end in childhood.

Research from interpersonal neurobiology, a field dedicated to studying how the brain grows and changes based on our relationships, shows us what plenty of us already knew: the people around us arouse our nervous systems for better and for worse.[2] Our spouses soothe *and* infuriate us. Our children delight *and* disappoint us. Our coworkers support *and* aggravate us.

Every single relationship "problem" on the planet comes down to difference, the complicated duality between independence and dependence. It's like our brains are saying, "I really want to be connected to you and there's just one simple catch: I decide how we do things around here."

For example, with couples, it is common that one person might expect words of affirmation when they are feeling sad or low. However, the other partner might believe that helping around the house (e.g., cleaning up, doing dishes) is the way to express love and support when their partner is sad. Both are perfectly acceptable ways to express love, but couples can feel deeply disconnected when they desire different "brands" of love.

If you lead a team, it can look like this: I'm super happy to be working on this project with you. This project is quite complex, and I truly could never do it without your expertise, too. I'm just going to need you to understand that I have some big opinions and, if we can't agree, we'll just be sure to do it my way.

In your parenting it can look like this: I love you so much, child, that I know what is best for you so now, here, eat this food, wear these clothes, and do these activities. No, not those ones. These ones.

Notice, too, how destructive the consequences are if you don't understand what the brain is doing. For example, I work with parents of teenagers who commonly say, "My child does not respect me," to which the child emphatically responds, "I *do* respect you! I just don't like math."

It may sound odd to say but neurobiology offers deep hope for the redemption and protection of all your relationships. If you can see, for example, that your child's preferences and non-preferences are just the brain's drive for independence and not a rejection of you, then you don't need to punish yourself with painful stories about how they don't respect or value you. They're literally doing what their brain is designed to do. It's normal human behavior.

When people come to work with me, they often come because people in their life aren't behaving as they wish people were behaving. They often start their conversation with me by saying, "I have a problem . . ."

This is the wrong frame.

You don't have a problem; you have a relationship. All meaningful relationships invariably produce this type of tension. In fact, the more meaningful the relationship, the more tension you'll likely feel.

The quality of the relationships you lead—at work, at home, and in your community—depend on whether you direct the energy of difference, always born in the tension of dependence and independence, toward a place of pain or a place of power. If you desire to create powerful relationships, you need to understand how to lead through the tension that these two competing neurobiological drives invariably produce in your relationships. This section of the book offers you three neuroenergetic codes that will empower you to harness emotional energies in service of your most powerful relationships:

- **Quit commanding:** How to release ineffective command-and-control styles of leading

- **Unleash your magnetism:** How to create your own brand of effortless leadership

- **Build a relationship from the future:** How to design your most powerful relationships at work and at home

Let's get into it.

Code 6: Quit Commanding

*How to release ineffective
command-and-control styles of leading*

Command energy is an extremely common energy in work, parenting, romantic relationships, educational systems, and even on social media. Command energy is when you try to control other people's energy—their behaviors, thoughts, and feelings—so you don't have to exert energy to change your own. It's the energy of "you do what I say so I don't have to be different." This code shows you how to stop using this energy so you can build more powerful, dynamic, and interconnected relationships.

Command energy is great in theory: if I can just get *you* to be different so I can have what *I* want, that would be energetically efficient. Theory aside, command energy does not work in thriving, dynamic relationships. In today's complex and fast-moving organizations and households, command energy rejects deeply interconnected relationships because it blocks equity. Commanding other people to behave in ways that aligns with your interests while denying theirs works against the fundamental design of their brain's drive for independence.

When I help people resolve pain in their relationships, I immediately look for where command energetics are at play. A few examples will help you see it clearly:

- **Corporate work:** In my corporate work, I commonly hear managers say they're stressed because they don't have enough "self-starters" on their team. But when I analyze their interactions, these managers are often sending conflicting energetic signals by, for example, asking too many questions, checking in too much, giving too much advice, or holding too many meetings. On multiple occasions, I've heard managers effectively say to their staff, "I want you to take total leadership on this project—just make sure you run it by me first." This is what I call "an energetic zero"—the messages cancel each other out as people, in confusion, wonder: "Wait, am I supposed to be self-starting or permission-seeking?" They're energetic opposites!

- **Parenting:** When children begin to develop healthy independence from their parents, this can be stressful and unwanted for parents. However, when parents don't create space for their children's emerging independence, it creates significant pain for their children. I worked with a mother and young adult daughter who were having conflict in their relationship. The mother claimed she wanted her daughter to move out of the house, but then she would send contradictory and controlling messages like: "What if you lose your job and can't afford the rent?" or "It's time for you to go, but it's gonna be too much for me to take care of this big house alone." The daughter was mired in a stressful swirl of wanting her independence, not feeling confident about her independence, and not wanting to abandon her mother.

- **Educational settings:** In school systems, I work with educators to design neuropsychologically informed approaches to education. Students are often encouraged to express their individual strengths, but then denied opportunities to explore these interests. For example, some students may have a clear preference for learning automotive or culinary skills but may be required to take traditional courses that do not match their skill sets or interests.

- **Love:** Long-term romantic love is the most complex relationship of all. Nowhere is the tension between dependence and independence greater. I once had a couple call an emergency session with me. They went out for what they envisioned would be a romantic picnic. However, on the walk to their picnic spot, they got into a fierce fight over proper ways to walk to a picnic. One of them was walking at a pace that did not feel romantic enough for the other. The need for choice and the need for connection—independence and dependence—clash so clearly in this example. The whole reason they wanted to have this picnic was to be connected, but then differences in individual preferences about walking to the picnic became so intense, it ruined the event.

Notice in these examples how the energies cancel themselves out. In each scenario, someone is communicating "I want you to be you" while simultaneously communicating "Just make sure I approve first!" It's like asking people to "Start! No, wait; stop! No, start!"— and then wondering why the whole thing feels like it doesn't have any momentum.

You might think that these scenarios seem outlandish—that, for example, you would never insist that someone walk to a picnic in a certain way. But when we feel rattled, we all overuse these ineffective command energies. I once got mad at someone for refusing to use a specific adjective to describe a project I was working on. It's a dark tale involving dictionaries and lots of debate about the meaning of words. 0/5 stars. Do not recommend. The point here is that I cannot stress enough how alive and powerful command energy is in nearly all relationships. Command energy is like gravity—so ubiquitous it's hardly noticed, but there it is, nonetheless, having a damn profound effect on our lives.

Let's run a quick test I call "energetic tugs-of-war." Have you ever, in the face of someone's disagreement with you, repeatedly:

- insisted that you were right while they insisted you were wrong?

- tried to prove them wrong?

- told them they "just didn't get it" or they "just didn't understand"?

- withdrawn from interacting with them? For example, did you refuse to call them back or avoid seeing them because it made you too frustrated that they didn't agree with you?

- given advice and gotten upset when they didn't take it?

- tried convincing them to be interested in something they clearly communicated they weren't? For example, do you say things like, "Just give it another try and I *know* you'll like it"?

- tried explaining why your way was the "best" way? For example, have you repetitively tried to make the case that your idea is the most logical, efficient, or socially responsible?

All these examples represent command energy. I call them "energetic tugs-of-war" because you can you see how, in each case, you're trying to pull the energy one way, while the other person yanks the energy back the other way. The problem with tugs-of-war is that everyone expends a ton of energy but nobody goes anywhere. Here's the thing: when you find yourself stuck in a tug-of-war, it's because you've lost your hold on your own power. At its core, what you're really communicating is: "I don't feel confident believing what I believe, thinking what I think, or doing what I do until *you* get over here with me, on my side, exactly as I require."

Now, you might be tempted to protest, "But my way *is* better; I *am* right." What I'm about to say is a tough weight for a lot of people to lift, but it's a weight that divides the emotionally average from the emotionally exceptional: unless you are talking about patently obvious objective facts (e.g., what day of the week it is; what time the invite said; what time the doctor's appointment is), there is no room for "being right" in powerful relationships. Decide: Do you want to be right—or do you want to be powerful?

Free Yourself from Your Energetic Tug-of-War

In a tug of war, people expend enormous amounts of energy and hardly move. But the only way for a tug-of-war to go on and on is if you and the other person have roughly the same energy. In other words, if your energy is either more powerful or weaker than mine, the tug of war is over in an instant. If you have *ongoing* stalemates or back-and-forths with your coworkers, stakeholders, children, partners, or people on social media that are driving you up a wall, I want to gently suggest it's because you're an energetic match for the very thing you claim is driving you bananas.

The great news is you can end these cycles of relational pain in a heartbeat. What's the fastest way to end a tug-of-war? Drop the rope.

Too often, we stay locked into these exhausting back-and-forths about who's more right, better, or smarter. But in this game, everyone ends up a loser. Command energy suffocates relationships because, from cradle to grave, human beings do not want to feel yanked around. Maybe you're starting to protest, "But why do *I* have to drop the rope? Why can't *they* drop the rope?" It may seem like dropping the rope is dropping out. Giving up. Losing.

It's not, though. The conversation we're having is about elite emotional power, uncommonly emotionally intelligent leadership. Look around you: so many people are locked in exhausting battles about who's more right, and all it produces is interpersonal destruction. What this tells you is that your willingness to voluntarily drop the rope isn't a sign of weakness. It's a total power move.

It's tough to expand beyond our view of what is "right." In fact, I don't know if there's anything harder than admitting that your way of doing, thinking, or being might not be the only way. That's precisely what makes this so emotionally powerful. Letting go of being right does not mean constantly capitulating to the opinions of people around you. It means you no longer require other people's approval to affirm what you already know to be true. It means you no longer feel threatened by their natural tendency to experience the world as they do. From this emotional posture, you lead people to the greatest relationships of all—relationships where they can be both connected and free.

You might still think that command energy works just fine. After all, there are plenty of examples of it. However, if you look closely, you will see that command energy does not allow you to reach your full leadership potential. As you work to loosen your grip on being right, it can be motivating to realize that if you insist on commanding others, you will be limited by the type and number of people you can hold in your relationships. Consider the example of Marc, a tech company executive.

Marc was whip-smart and fast-talking with a personality like a trial lawyer. He said that his leadership strategy was to debate people until they agreed with him. While this style worked early in his career, as he started to work at some very successful startups, he noted that the "strength of people's wills and intelligence got sharper." In other words, Marc's old strategies of debating people until they capitulated no longer worked.

"I was so frustrated because I felt like there was this energetic block, like I could always advance until a certain point and then the whole thing would come crashing down," Marc said to me. "This made me think I needed to prove myself even more—so I tried even harder to tell people how to do it. I was determined to be the smartest guy in the room."

After getting fired from three jobs, Marc realized that his constant need to be right wasn't advancing him; it was ruining him. After some deep reflection, Marc had a profound realization: His need to be right meant he needed other people to be in lockstep with his thinking.

He realized that if he needed this level of agreement, he could only lead a few people. Given the career ambitions he had, there was no way he could realistically expect to get dozens, or hundreds, to be in perfect lockstep with him.

Marc started to realize that his need for other people's approval was the boss of him. "I started to see that as long as I needed everyone to agree with me before I could lead, then I wasn't leading much at all." Marc recalled, "Once it clicked, it forever changed the way I led."

When he was able to release his need to be right, his emotional power exploded—and so did his career. He landed at one of the largest, most successful tech companies in the world, overseeing one of their largest divisions. Early in his career, Marc thought commanding others was a powerful leadership strategy, but it was his willingness to quit commanding that helped him become the emotionally intelligent leader he aspired to be.

There's no shame at all in command energy. The whole reason any of us even know command energy in the first place is because it was taught to us in childhood—the period when your brain was encoding its fundamental lessons about what leadership feels like. Do you recognize any of these commands?

Sit down.	Not now.
Stand up.	Tell them you're sorry.
Stop it.	Keep your hands to yourself.
Go to bed.	Be quiet.
Eat that.	

I'm guessing they're familiar phrases. In some cases, command energy can be miraculously adaptive. For example, if someone was about to get hit by a car and you screamed, "Get out of the way!" or if your kid was about to drink Lysol and you yelled, "Put that down!," these are effective uses of command energy. But command energy has its limits.

Because you're invested in the most emotionally powerful expression of your leadership, you'll want a more sophisticated repertoire of interpersonal energies. There's an increasing cultural awareness that command-and-control relationships are not emotionally powerful. But, like any problem, until you understand the true root from which it grows, it will persist.

The root of command energy is your lack of trust.

You only seek to control what you do not trust. Do you check your car's brake system before you leave your garage or ask to inspect a plane's engine before it takes off? Probably not, because you trust those things so much it doesn't even occur to you to question them.

You might think you command other people because you don't trust *them*. But the truth is you don't trust *yourself*.

- You don't trust that *you'll* be OK if people don't do it your way, so you command through criticism.

- You don't trust that it's safe for *you* to make mistakes so you command through micromanagement.

- You don't trust that *your* explanation was sufficient so you command through overexplaining.

- You don't trust that *you* have enough time, so you command by badgering people to give you answers more quickly.

- You don't trust that *you've* already proven yourself, so you command by demanding more from the people around you.

Consider Jan, who came to work with me because she was getting clear feedback from her staff that she was micromanaging them. Her team complained that they felt stifled and controlled. Jan explained to me that she prided herself on delivering top-notch quality, admitting that her style was "demanding."

But as we went deeper, it turned out that Jan was so demanding because she was terrified of losing control. Although she had achieved all that she had set out to accomplish—she had the family and the high-powered career—Jan admitted she often felt more overwhelmed than empowered. She lamented feeling like she was always on her heels, noting that she was losing control as a corporate leader, mother, and wife. Jan struggled with her home life, realizing that she often found herself dreading the weekend. She half-joked, "I like work because it's the only place where people actually listen to me."

Jan started to realize that the more overwhelmed she felt in her life, especially her life at home, the more she tried to regain her emotional balance by controlling her staff. It wasn't until Jan started to address all the places where she was "leaking" energy—losing her sense of control and safety—that she was able to restore herself to a healthy balance.

Exercise: Plug Energetic Leaks

To quit commanding, try this exercise to plug energetic leaks. Energetic leaks are the places where you lose control of your emotional energy. So long as you feel you cannot reasonably control yourself, you will seek to control others. If you can plug these leaks, you'll have less of a desire to control other people, empowering you to show up as stronger across your relationships. I'll show you a four-step exercise and then give you two examples to see it in action, one in table format and one in narrative form.

1. Think of someone you've spent the most energy trying to convince, control, persuade, influence, or motivate. This can be *anyone*, from an obstinate coworker who massively annoys you to a parent you've exhausted yourself trying to educate about the error of their ways. Pick someone you've really invested a ton of energy in because I want to show you how to heal this relationship in the most upstream way.

2. Identify two to three character traits about this person that deeply pain you. For example, maybe they're critical and volatile.

3. Identify where you leak these energies into your relationships. In other words, where in your life do you possess the *same*

energy you resent being inflicted upon you? For example, if you chose critical as the characteristic that bothers you in another person, ask: "Where in my life do I hurt others because *I am* critical?" Notice if you already have a defensive reaction to this step of the exercise, thinking "*I'm* not critical; *they* are!" If you are pained by someone else's criticisms, you too exhibit this energy. You cannot recognize what you do not know—and you cannot know what you do not possess. Perhaps you know your own energy under a different name like demanding, precise, picky, difficult to please, intense, finicky, fussy, or exacting. But somewhere you are transmitting the same brand of energy that has pained you. Identify where it is. Blind spots exist and defensive mechanisms are real. If you struggle, ask people who are close to you where they see this energy emanating from you and leaking into your relationships.

4. Heal the energy where it leaks from you. After you've determined where you're critical, take the necessary steps to stop the behavior. Often criticism does not show up in the same situation where you're pained by it. For example, if your father was critical, you may not be critical toward your father, but you may be critical toward your spouse, children, and employees. Heal it there—and you will see that the energy that bothered you no longer will pain you.

If you can learn to quit your command energy, you will see far-reaching positive results in your relationships. Mostly, you will start to feel more *self*-confident. The following two examples show you this in action.

The first, in table 4, is from Marti, a successful solopreneur and loving mother. Despite her success, she frequently felt judged by her own mother. To combat this pain, Marti reported that she spent copious amounts of energy trying to convince, inspire, and persuade her mother that she was successful enough, smart enough, and worthy enough. Table 4 shows the steps Marti took to plug her energetic leaks.

TABLE 4

Your energetic leaks

Steps to plug your energetic leaks	Marti's case
Identify your leak: name who you've spent energy trying to convince, control, persuade, etc.	Marti's mother
Name their top quality that pains you.	Judgmental
Identify where you leak the same energy you say pains you from another.	Marti realized she was frequently judging others (e.g., their work, their appearance, why they shouldn't have made as much money as they had, why their business should be more successful than it was, etc.)
Heal your leak.	Marti worked to stop judging others. As she became more accepting of others, her *self*-acceptance also increased. As her *self*-acceptance became more powerful, she had less of a need for her mother's acceptance and she subsequently became less affected by her mother's judgments.

The second example is the case of Ruben, a VP of sales at a manufacturing company. Although he generally liked his job, Ruben was so stressed by one volatile coworker that he thought regularly about finding a new job. But the idea of leaving his job bothered him. Ruben ultimately decided that before taking that step, he would first try to stop getting triggered, frightened, or anxious around this coworker.

I told Ruben I had good news—that he could take back his emotional power. All he had to do was stop being volatile. At first, Ruben was confused. It was his colleague who was volatile, he insisted. But soon, Ruben remembered his turbulent relationship with his mother-in-law and his neighbors. He noted that whenever his mother-in-law would come over he would bicker with her, and his wife described his behavior as moody. He also realized he had an unpredictable relationship with his neighbors. Ruben regularly argued with them and, on several occasions, he threatened to involve lawyers over relatively minor offenses.

Even though Ruben's presenting complaint was about his coworker, he agreed to first focus on cleaning up his energetic leaks around his mother-in-law and neighbors. As he became more emotionally possessed, he was pleasantly surprised to learn that his relationship with his coworker barely bothered him. Why? Because to heal up the relationship with his mother-in-law and neighbors, he needed to become more emotionally powerful—more centered and more *self*-supported. And the thing about energy is that it does not belong to any specific situation. When you heal it over there, you heal it everywhere.

Drop the rope. Let the war be over.

Code 7:
Unleash Your Magnetism

How to create your most effortless leadership

When you quit commanding, you free up energy in your relationships, allowing you to unleash a more powerful energy: the energy of your magnetism. Magnetic leadership is when others follow you because they are attracted to the power of your example. This is the most powerful way to lead because it's the most aligned with how your brain operates. People are connected to you not because you insist, but because they choose—it's a neurological win-win. This code shows you how to radiate a more magnetic energy in your relationships.

Magnetic energy is powerful because it strikes the optimal balance between the brain's drive for both dependence and independence. We all know of leaders who magnetize others with their genuine energy for the mission they serve. They're not thinking about controlling us—obsessed with our work, what we're doing, and what we're not. Instead, they're focused on the larger mission and, as an effect, we can't help but be turned on by their energy.

When your actions arise from the right energy—when you act inspired because you *feel* inspired or when you act generously because you *feel* generous—relationships are strengthened. Kids listen, employees believe, customers engage, and partners trust. Whether you steward people at work, online, or at home, it's when people choose to follow your lead *because they want to* that you'll know you've built the most powerful relationships of all.

Here's an example from Miles, a partner in a consulting firm who had success as a leader, building a team with strong morale while increasing revenue by approximately 1,000 percent in less than two years. Miles says the main reason he's had so much success is because he's energized by a collective mission—by binding his team under a bigger vision that belongs to them all. Miles explains that deep success came when "we removed this concept of there being a task that had to be done and started focusing on a mission we desired to achieve together. It turns out the more I genuinely believe in that common mission, the more I become the leader people *want* to follow."

Miles explains that part of his success—part of his magnetism—is that he doesn't try to take credit. He says, "I take no credit for anything. In fact, I've had my own personal sales targets removed because I said if I'm taking sales credit, I have to fight with my team over what gets allocated to me over a deal, and that's not how you build a team. So I had my team structured in such a way that I have a zero sales target and I am measured only on the success of my team as a whole. When I first tried to structure my team like this, it was unheard of—but the results have been staggering."

Miles's approach allowed him to create an effortless brand of leadership. By creating an environment in which people had *both* personal agency and collective meaning, Miles's team followed him because they wanted to. Your job as a leader at work and at home is to create an environment that allows people to tap into the full range of their emotional power—to access the power of things like belonging, excitement, growth, safety, authenticity, trust, and boundaries. You are the emotional standard to which your people calibrate. Your ability to offer the right energies to your people depends on your ability to access them within yourself. That's precisely why the first five codes started by building *your* emotional power. Mastery of those five codes will serve as a sound foundation for strengthening your magnetic energy.

This neuroenergetic code reminds you: you cannot give what you do not have. How can you offer the energy of belonging when you don't feel like you belong? How can you lead with the energy of enthusiasm when you're exhausted? How can you show people you trust them when you don't even trust yourself? How can you create a feeling of safety when you don't feel safe?

Arguably, the greatest barrier to the full energetic range of your leadership is your decision to prioritize other people's opinions over the truth of your own energy. If you desire to create environments where people feel empowered to be not just popular but true, you must first be willing to show yourself—even at the risk of disappointing others. Take Greg, the CEO of a large consulting firm who oversees thousands of employees. With a strong reputation as a leader who is both well-liked and well-respected, Greg is a magnetic leader, someone others want to follow. Greg specifically credits his leadership success to the energy of his authenticity—his own willingness to repeatedly show up as he is. "With me, what you see is what you get. I see lots of C-suite leaders whose authenticity meter gets stripped away slowly as they ascend this corporate ladder. They don't actually know it's happening to them. I think you're subconsciously trying to manage an image of what you're supposed to be like and, for me, that's a recipe for struggling to connect."

To be an authentic leader, Greg realized there were powerful energies that must be resisted: "There's this gravitational force that wants you to spend time with only senior people. So I fight that gravity with intention every day, every week, every month, every year." In a leadership landscape where it's so easy to try to perform for other people's approval, Greg attributes much of his success to doing the *opposite*: He actively does *not* try to be liked.

> What my wife would tell you is that one of the things that
> makes me capable of leading a big team, particularly in

moments of pain, is that I don't agonize over what people think. I am not worried about winning a popularity contest. I accept that the burden of leadership comes with the ultimate responsibility to make a set of decisions that are complicated, nuanced. They're not 100/0 calls. They're 51/49 calls. . . . I am perfectly comfortable that when I make a decision and I know that some significant portion of a population might not agree with the decision, that's not a sleep loss moment for me.

By not claiming your authenticity, you risk feeling in danger even when, by all objective measures, you have achieved significant success. Consider Bevvy, the founder and CEO of a highly successful tech start-up. Despite her success, Bevvy felt insecure. Although she couldn't exactly put her finger on the issue, she was perpetually worried that it was only a matter of time before she was "found out" and excluded from the business she created. "I often don't feel like I belong in the house I built," she said to me.

At her core, Bevvy was afraid of being seen as not good enough, but her fear masqueraded as aggression. With a reputation for being terse and critical, Bevvy had created a team with low metrics of engagement and belonging. Through our work, it became clear that many of the behaviors Bevvy's team found *offensive* were things she was doing as a form of *defense*. For example, she realized her rough communication style was mostly a form of self-protection. She feared that if she was too gentle or too open, others would be able to get too close and hurt her. Bevvy began to see self-acceptance, not as some esoteric goal, but as a core leadership mandate: until she knew how to accept herself, she could not meaningfully lead a culture of belonging.

If you feel like the power of your magnetism is not as powerful as you know it could be, chances are high it's because you're cutting yourself off from the full range of your magnetic energy. Remember our definition of emotional power: it's your refusal to divide yourself from yourself; it's your wholeness. When you are emotionally whole—when you honor the fullness of who you actually are—your emotional leadership becomes inevitable. People's deep and universal desire is to be accepted for who they are—*to be worthy as they are.* When you lead from a place of your own emotional empowerment, you become the evidence of the thing people want most in their lives: access to their own power.

To access a more magnetic energy, place your focus on the only thing you could ever control anyway—yourself. There's great news for you here. It's energizing and freeing when you realize you're free from the exhausting energy of commanding, controlling, convincing, demanding, engaging, or motivating others. Think about how much exhaustion you have experienced in your body trying to convince, influence, persuade, coax, prompt, entice, cajole, or motivate people. *It does not need to be this hard.* Your leadership *can* feel more effortless, pleasurable, and effective when you realize that your job isn't to motivate others. It's to be motivated and trust that others will find you motivating.

Your job is not to be inspiring. Your job is to be inspired and trust that others will find you inspiring. Your job is not to worry about influencing others. Your job is to improve your ability to influence yourself.

Your job was never to lead them. The command-and-control paradigm of leadership was always a setup, a bad design that cannot sustainably work based on how we now know human brains work. To spend all your energy leading in a way the brain doesn't support is a fool's errand.

So what *is* your job?

To lead yourself. And when you lead yourself, the right people will follow.

A Real-Life Example of Unleashing Your Magnetism

I was recruited to assist the executive team at a large nonprofit, one with an exceptional mission, offering technological solutions to some of the world's most vulnerable people through innovative technology. These leaders were bright, motivated, and cared deeply about their organization. Despite their competence and energizing mission, the organization had abysmal employee engagement.

When starting a project like this, I like to know where people's heads are—how they're conceptualizing the pain in their organizations—so I asked these leaders, "What ideas have you been tossing around to solve this problem?" They rattled off a list of initiatives that included staff reorganizations, getting rid of managers they saw as problematic (but who were well-liked by the staff), and giving people rewards, like gift cards and bonuses.

But there are more emotionally powerful places to start. In the examples the executive team initially offered, can you see that the most fundamental energetic impulse behind each of these initiatives is: "How do I get these people to behave how I want without changing me at all?"

There's no good or bad in this. These leaders are not bad for wanting their staff to be engaged, motivated, and inspired without having to significantly change their own behavior. They're human. Change is hard precisely because it's energy intensive; it's biologically natural to hope others change so we don't have to. But the problem, as you know by now, is that it doesn't work.

Across all relationships, it's common for us to demand that others change so we don't have to do *our* emotional work.

- In organizations, this can sound like, "What can we do to make these employees more productive?" or "How can we get people to be more innovative around here?"

- With parents, this can sound like: "How do I get my children to listen?" Or "How do I make my kid to do these things that she doesn't like doing—like eating these foods or hanging out with different friends?"

- In schools, this can sound like: "How do we make these students less distracted?" Or "How do we get these kids to care more—to be more engaged and less overwhelmed?"

- With couples, it's "How can I make my partner see that what he is doing is wrong?" Or "How can I get my partner to see that how she's acting isn't right?"

The full energetic impulse behind a question like "How can I get my kid to listen?" is often more accurately stated as "How can I make my kid do the thing I want her to do that she has repeatedly shown me she does not want to do?"

When the question is asked in its emotionally honest form, the answer is clear: You cannot.

It's a total power move to meet your relationships in the energy of what they already are because it's only from the point of honesty that true change takes hold. You cannot cause the sensation of wanting in someone else's nervous system. And, for the love of God, if you cannot do this for your own children, the very people that emerged from your flesh, you cannot do it for anyone else. It's strange how much energy we've put into creating hierarchical systems of leadership that gave most of us the *hallucination* that we could control other people's desires and behavior. Many of us have been set up to confuse our sources of power; we insist we have control over other people while forgoing the profound agency we have over our own energy.

Back to the executive team at the nonprofit. When I asked them about their own levels of inspiration, motivation, and engagement, I heard comments from leaders who were exhausted, frustrated, and confused. In private one-on-one meetings, several leaders cried, lamenting how overwhelmed they were.

In group meetings with the full executive team, these leaders all expressed their dismay with some of their top managers. However, it was only when I met with each executive leader alone that they privately told me how upset they were with many of their co-executive leaders. Several members of the executive team even confided in me that they were seriously considering leaving.

These leaders were lost in the pain of their own confusion and conflict because they were a match for it. In other words, the reason they thought the organization was awash in confusion and conflict is because *they* were awash in confusion and conflict.

If this seems too out there for you, it may seem more reasonable if we take this same logic and apply it to a romantic couple. Partners in conflict are very often both the receiver *and* the giver of the same energy. For example, when one person in the couple says, "My partner makes me feel like I'm not good enough" or "I'm rejected by my partner," it is nearly always the case that the other person in the couple also feels rejected. Because rejection is such a painful human experience, people then start behaving in defensive ways that subsequently reinforce the very system creating the rejection.

In the case of the nonprofit, these leaders had forgotten their power. They had forgotten that *they* were the magnets to which other people are attracted or from which they are repelled. The low energy they possessed had everything to do with the dynamics they were so committed to changing. My central task was to strengthen their magnetic energy.

Our work began by ceasing downstream efforts about the staff and focusing on the connection between these leaders with their own emotional power. First, I helped them see that the conflict they were having with their key managers was simply a mirror of the conflict they were having among themselves, and that they could not expect to meaningfully defuse the energy of conflict with their topline managers while also having intra-executive team fights. To make a clear analogy: High conflict parents who constantly fight with each other often also have distress in their relationship with their children. Pain seeps. Relationships with our children don't improve while painful energies, feelings of stress, distrust, and rage, gush within us. Inevitably we bring the fullness of ourselves to our relationships—the only question is if we're going to be conscious of our energy or not.

As the executive team started to see the clear impact their intra-executive conflict was having across the organizational system, they became more willing to engage with one another more transparently and collaboratively. This sense of connection—the sense they were now all naming the foundational emotional problem and committed to resolving it collectively—improved the situation immensely. After we defused their intra-executive conflict, these leaders realized they wanted to have more honest dialogues with their key managers. They started weekly working groups. But to build human relationships, it was vital to prioritize *informal* interactions that are hallmarks of strong relationships. Research shows high performing teams prioritize informal interactions and time bonding over nonwork topics.[1] So, these executives made it a point to casually drop by managers' offices, regularly pick up the phone to talk informally about issues, and genuinely take interest in their managers' nonwork lives.

There was one manager with whom executive leadership had a particularly strained relationship. When I first started working with the executive team, they swore that this manager "hated" them. But hate is always the defense of fear. Chances were high that this manager was afraid of the executive team. Fear often looks like aggression.

We explicitly committed to assume good intent—that this manager was a hard worker who was committed to the organization and wanted a healthy professional relationship with the executive team. Their next act of leadership was not to wait around and hope this manager had a change of heart, but to take initiative.

One of the executive leaders was especially emotionally powerful. She made it a point to regularly pop into this manager's office. At first it *was* painful—it was awkward, stressful, and stilted—but soon, the executive and the manager were regularly stopping by each other's office, sometimes even bringing each other coffee. This may seem like a small gesture, but it was a profound signal of how much the energy had changed when the executive team started to worry less about the behavior of others and think more about how they wanted to show up in the energy of their own leadership.

People felt the change. What was most impressive to my clients was that the more they *embodied*—instead of demanded—the type of leadership they hoped to see, the more it showed up. As topline managers started to feel the genuine concern of the executive team, they reflected this energy toward their own teams. There was an increase in the number of formal events for communications, like town halls.

Even more importantly for the organizational culture was the increase in small, informal interactions that signaled a powerful rise in trust: a comment here, a decision to ask someone for their opinion there, a willingness to change plans to accommodate others' schedules. Employee engagement scores rose. Unleashing the power of the executive team's magnetism did far more than any gift cards or personnel firing could have.

There's an emotional math to your relationships. If you change a little, the relationship will change a little. If you change a lot, the relationship will change a lot. It is impossible for you to meaningfully change and for the relationship to stay the same.

Notice that when you try to control other people, it's because you've lost hold of your own power. It's only when you're (often unconsciously) consumed by your own painful emotions—like anxiety, fear, and doubt—that you attempt to control others.

Why do you do this?

Because you've spent your entire life attempting to use other people's behavior to regulate your own nervous system, a code programmed into you in childhood.

Leave childish things to children. As an adult, when you insist *they* do, think, or feel things *you* want, this isn't leadership—it's codependency. All codependency means is you don't know how to regulate your own nervous system so you try to get somebody else's behavior to do it for you.

When you're ready for new levels of emotional power, it's time to trust. Trust yourself. Trust the process. Trust that people who want to be a part of your life will be—not because they are coerced, but because they choose. Lead yourself and trust that those who are meant to connect to you will.

For many of us who have rooted the success of our leadership in our overdoing, overthinking and overdelivering, this level of trust can seem so foreign that it can feel terrifying. To use less emotionally accurate words, like "uncomfortable," "ineffective," or "challenging," belies the (often) unconscious but deeper fear that if you stop trying to overcontrol, you will be harmed.

Soothe yourself with this: It's safe to let all that controlling go because it wasn't working anyway. The quality of human relationships exists to the degree that people connect to you through their own free will. Can you command a lover to love you? Can you demand a friend enjoy you? Can you require a child respect you?

No, no, and no.

Once you realize that control over other people was a costly illusion, one that led you to give away so much of your precious energy, you can simply release the old ways of leading that didn't work anyway. Just like it's easy to let go of a lottery ticket when you know your numbers won't be called, it's easier to let go of old command-based paradigms of leadership when you realize they packed no power at all. And when you release this impotent energy, you create space to unleash a powerful asset in your leadership: Your magnetism.

Exercise: Making Magnetic Relationships

Your magnetism relies, most fundamentally, on the way you carry your own energy. To strengthen your magnetism, reflect on the following groups of questions. Grab a journal and a quiet space. Get yourself a room-temperature glass of water or an herbal tea, or some other comforting beverage. Take ten deep breaths to really calm your nervous system, emphasizing your exhales. Now freewrite—don't overthink—your answers to these questions.

I call this making magnetic relationships. To strengthen your magnetism, reflect on these questions. Answer the questions that resonate with you; some will and some won't. You don't have to answer all of them. Review the list and then more deeply examine the ones that resonate. Answer gently but honestly.

SELF-EMPOWERMENT
- What are the ways a fuller expression of your power scares you (e.g., more people to rely on you; more people to disappoint; more people you need to give explanations)?

- People project onto their leaders. What scares you about how other people might project on you as you become increasingly powerful (e.g., maybe they think that you're now too controlling, or that you don't really care about them, or that you don't have time for them, or that you use people to get where you are, or that you only care about your image, etc.)?

- Think back to your source code—to your early childhood lessons. What lessons did your parents teach you about power? For example, how did you see your parents act or hear your parents talk about people in authority or "people in power?" How does that affect your relationship with your leadership today?

- Is there more untapped potential inside of you? If yes, when will you be ready to access it? What precisely would need to happen before you are willing to unleash it?

- Who needs to give you permission to access deeper levels of your emotional power?

BELONGING

- Where do you feel like it's time to reclaim more belonging in your life? For example, are there spaces in your life that you feel you don't belong as much as you wish?

- Do you still feel like you belong *even when* you feel misunderstood? Or do you need to feel perfectly understood in order to feel like you belong?

- What are the situations where you tend to exclude yourself? What are the stories you tend to tell yourself about how other people don't want you there? How do you sometimes become an agent of your own exclusion?

- Are there certain people you don't feel like you belong around? Why?

- Go back to your source code. What lessons did your parents give you about how and when you belonged? Was your belonging conditional? If so, how?

AUTHENTICITY AND TRANSPARENCY

- What is your greatest fear about being fully seen in your leadership? For example, are you afraid that you will be seen as incompetent, unwanted, or unworthy? Do you worry about being smothered by other people's incessant needs? Do you fear becoming unrelatable to certain people?

- What things do you least want people to know about you? If they knew those things, how do you believe it would affect your leadership? What would happen if you allowed those parts of you to be seen?

BOUNDARIES

- Where do you fail to hold your boundaries?

- Do you tell people to rest but then fail to follow your own advice? Why?

- Where are you too available? Why?

- Where are you not available enough? Why?

- Are you able to say "no"? Where do you notice that it's especially hard to say no?

RELATIONSHIPS WITH OTHERS

- Where do you trust others on your team? Where does that trust end? What specific situations do you find yourself overchecking, overasking, or overmanaging?

- Where do you generally believe that people will support or help you?

- Where do you generally believe that people will disappoint or harm you?

RELATIONSHIP TO YOURSELF

- Would *you* follow you? Are *you* inspired by you? Are *you* turned on by your own life—do *you* feel alive, creative, and empowered? Why or why not? Look deeper. What patterns do you see in the moments when you like who you are? What patterns trigger you to lose hold of the person you want to be?

- What are your patterns that block a fuller range of your leadership power? For example, do you miss deadlines? Do you overwork on certain projects, exhaust yourself, and then fail to meet other commitments in your life? Do you fixate on readiness, the idea that you need more information before you can move forward?

- Do you genuinely like being in the presence of your own energy? Here are a couple of questions to test it:

  - If you were your own manager at work, what would it be like? Would you like working for you? What would be the good parts? The challenging parts?

  - If your child brought home a fiancé who was effectively you, what would be your reaction? Why? Would you be joyful or upset that they would be spending their life with someone who acts like you and treats people the way you treat people?

- How have you spent energy nurturing a respecting relationship with yourself? For example, do you almost always honor your commitments to yourself, even to small things? What are the reasons you break your commitments to yourself? How would you describe the quality of the intimacy you have with yourself? How do you soothe yourself?

If you deeply reflect on these questions, you will illuminate new levels of self-awareness. The foundational step to any type of psychological change is always awareness. Your task now is to move from awareness to action. To do this, simply select a target and do it. For example, if while reflecting on these questions, you realize you have particular trouble holding boundaries, select a target behavior that would provide you with evidence your boundaries are strengthening. Choose to do any activity that feels empowering to you—for example, ask today for one specific thing you want, say no three times this week, plan to politely leave two conversations that don't feel good to you—and then do it.

Your magnetism does not depend on outcomes so much as it relies on your energy. Strengthen your emotional power by using *all* of you. How effectively you influence others depends on how honestly you inspire yourself. When you start allowing yourself to be exactly what you are, you give other people permission to access what they ultimately want, too: themselves.

And this is the most magnetic energy of all.

Code 8:
Build a Relationship from the Future

How to design your most powerful relationships at work and at home

f your relationships don't feel as strong or rewarding as you would like, chances are it's because you don't have a clear vision for them. To build deeply successful relationships at work and at home, you can't just think about them as they presently stand. You need to envision them in the future.

Your relationships are energetic connections *over time*: people feel emotional energies around you, and you feel emotional energies around them. The time component is essential to your relationships, too. Your relationships with your team, partner, kids, friends, and, in many cases, clients and social media followers endure over the span of months, years, and even decades. If the time component is missing, you don't have a relationship; you have an interaction. You pass someone on the road; you speak to a store clerk. For your relationships to stay strong over time, you must train yourself to project how they will evolve through time. You do this by looking beyond whatever has occurred in the past and whatever is occurring in the present toward a more powerful vision of how you want your relationships to *feel in the future*.

The thing about time is that now always turns into later. If you don't position yourself to meet your relationship in the future, there is a good chance that—when later arrives—you will not have created the most powerful version of your relationship. In neuroenergetic code 2, we discussed the power of your patterns—the idea that your emotional power becomes stronger when you have a pattern fierce enough to support you through your pain. Notice, too, how cultural lore already enthusiastically embraces stories of *individuals* rising to meet a more powerful version of their future self.

Consider, for example, Michael Jordan. Arguably the best basketball player of all time, Jordan was cut from his high school basketball team. After learning he did not make the team, he went home, locked himself in his room, and cried. Quickly, though, he was able to look beyond his current circumstance and create a vision from the future—a projection, not of who he was but of who he had the potential to become. "Whenever I was working out and got tired and figured I ought to stop, I'd close my eyes and see that list in the locker room without my name on it," Jordan explained. "That usually got me going again."[1] Jordan describes how using his past emotional pain—his feelings of disappointment and rejection—catalyzed a powerful expansion in his future self. On the individual level, we both recognize the utility of and are inspired by stories of individuals creating, and then materializing, visions of their future self.

It's the same with relationships.

This code shows you how to create more powerful, energizing relationships with the people you care about—your kids, clients, partner, or team—by building a future vision of it.

Just like Michael Jordan might imagine himself sinking free throw after free throw, you build stronger relationships when you envision yourself being the person you desire to be in your relationships. It's not magic; it's neural conditioning. You're priming your nervous system to be in the optimal position to hold the emotional energy you desire, particularly under painful conditions. Visualization helps regulate levels of nervous system arousal to reduce ineffective behaviors and thoughts while increasing focus.[2] Visualization is so powerful that it's routinely used as an evidence-based strategy to help people recover from trauma and anxiety disorders.[3]

Scientific evidence and our everyday experiences show us that our future emotional states are not exactly predictable.[4] I'm sure you've had plenty of moments when you swore you were going to feel one thing and ended up feeling another. You were certain you're going to be in a good mood and you're not; you think you won't be annoyed, but you are. To overcome the unpredictability of the brain's emotional system, you must activate the power of your brain's visualization capabilities to train yourself to feel what you want to feel.

Let's do an activity. Choose any one relationship with another person that you desire to strengthen (e.g., your colleague, partner, team, clients, or kid). Now, quickly write down answers to the following questions. Don't overthink it; just write what comes to mind:

- What *specific* things will be happening in this relationship in the future?

- When you envision this relationship in the future, what *specific* feelings do you want to feel in your body when you're interacting in this relationship?

- Choose a time at some point in the future, like six months, one year, or ten years. When you imagine this relationship at that point in the future, what memories have you created together that you're incredibly proud of?

This is a powerful exercise, but when I first do it with people, they typically struggle to answer the questions. Interestingly, however, when I ask people if they have a future vision of other things—their career, their financial situation, the type of house they'll be living in, or even what will be happening in their kids' lives many years from now—it's common to hear people rattle off very precise descriptions. I once worked with a father who showed up to one of our sessions wearing a University of Michigan sweatshirt. I casually asked him if that's where he went to school. He said no, but it would be where his daughter was going. He then proceeded to enthusiastically tell me what she was going to study.

The child was eight weeks old.

While this well-intentioned father had a clear academic plan for his kid, when I asked him to describe to me his favorite memories that he and his daughter will have made by the time he dropped her off at her Michigan dorm room, he couldn't articulate much.

Note that if you struggle to articulate a precise future vision for your relationship, it's OK. In fact, it's good news because it means there are powerful, untapped strategies that await you.

To empower your relationships over time, it is important to hold a clear future vision of them. In my work with managers, parents, and couples, I've learned that operating our relationships without a future vision often creates two problems:

- You forget *your* power in *your* relationship.

- You (often unconsciously) believe the relationship's *future* potential is controlled by *past* experiences.

Remember Your Power as a Cocreator in Your Relationships

Relationships are, by their nature, cocreations. Often, when our relationships start to go off the rails, it's because we've forgotten our role as a cocreator. Whether with a coworker, our family, or our partner, it's easy to feel overwhelmed and even hopeless when things start to sour. In this helpless state, we plunge into a passive mentality where we see the relationship as something that is happening to us rather than an entity co-controlled by us. For example, when I'm working with leaders who have lost hold of their own power, it's common to hear them say something like, "This team is totally disengaged and the whole thing is pointless." When I work with couples who are demoralized by the state of their relationship, they often say things like, "My partner refuses to listen to me and it's hopeless." When I work with parents who feel helpless over the relationship with their child, they often say things like, "There's nothing I can do to get my kid to talk to me."

In moments like these, we lose our own agency, forgetting that *our* relationships invariably belong to *us*. We forget that our energy is so essential to the relationship that the relationship, quite literally, vanishes without our participation. All relationships aren't meant to last forever. Sometimes, it's time for relationships to end, and that's OK, too. Here, we're not focusing on relationships you want to end; we're talking about relationships you want to improve but can't figure out how. In these cases, your interpersonal power rises at warp speed when you remind yourself of a central truth: the quality of your relationships with others energetically mirrors your relationship with yourself.

In my work with teams and couples, when I gently ask them if they feel toward themselves the energy they're lamenting is missing in their relationships with others, the overwhelming answer is no. For example:

- A manager who's demoralized because her team isn't being creative often realizes that *she's* not feeling creative.

- A father who feels disrespected by his child's behavior toward him struggles to point to examples demonstrating how he respects *himself*.

- A wife who's heartbroken because she thinks her husband isn't madly in love with her has a very difficult time describing the ways in which she fiercely loves *herself*.

- An adult son, angry that no matter how hard he tries he never feels fully accepted by his parents, cannot produce evidence of his own *self*-acceptance.

The *only* way you access your relationship with others is through your own nervous system. This means the quality of your relationships with others is *always* mediated by the quality of your relationship with yourself. If you spend significant amounts of your life feeling bad in your own skin, it becomes a supremely difficult task for your external relationships to override the energy of your internal state. Of course, our social relationships have a profound impact on our quality of life.[5] But of all the relationships that shape your life, it's the one you have with yourself that's the most powerful.

There is an emotional math to your relationships. Just like when you change one variable in a mathematical equation and the answer changes, if you change *your* energy, the energy in the relationship *invariably* changes. To build a stronger relationship with others in the future, you first must build a more emotionally powerful relationship with yourself. You began this work in neuroenergetic code 6, where you plugged your energetic leaks. You looked for places where your fear about other people's negative energy (e.g., judgment or criticism) was a signpost, pointing you to the precise places where you could clean up this particular energy to become emotionally stronger. You continued this evolution in neuroenergetic code 7, identifying specific ways *you* block your wholeness in *your* relationships (e.g., the ways you divide yourself; the places you exclude yourself; the ways you ignore yourself). In this neuroenergetic code, we build on this momentum, helping you create your most powerful relationships through an exercise called "focusing on me to strengthen we."

If you want to create powerful relationships, here's one simple—and counterintuitive—thing you can do: stop fixating on the other person and start centering yourself.

When your nervous system gets triggered into a conflict state, it's easy to prioritize the destruction of others *over* empowerment of yourself. We obsess about *them*—perseverating on what they're doing, ruminating on how they're feeling. Conflict is an electric energy. The problem is when your brain is energized for combat it's not particularly forward-thinking. Given my work with high-conflict couples, I routinely see people destroy their own self-interest in the process of trying to injure another. I've had couples, in the heat of marital rage, post things on social media that led to the destruction of their *own* careers and social relationships. Similarly, I've had cofounders, at war with each other, sabotage their *own* business because they couldn't figure out how to get along with each other. When the conflict cooled, these people were immensely pained by their behavior—embarrassed and remorseful—but the damage had already been done.

There's a painful immediacy to conflict—a feeling of intense anxiety, stress, or fear that makes you forget *your* future. You strengthen yourself and protect your relationships when, in the heat of conflict, you forget the other person and start centering yourself. In other words, if your coworker, client, spouse, or kid is driving you bonkers, don't worry about them. Instead start obsessing about your future vision for your own life.

It may seem odd, somehow self-centered or egotistical, to center yourself in your relationship. But the opposite is true. When you approach your relationships from a place of your own emotional empowerment, you build deeply authentic, connected, mutually enriched relationships.

Exercise: Focusing on Me to Strengthen We

Before we do this exercise, know that you must do this this work *before* your nervous system gets triggered. When you're deeply triggered—enraged, upset, or flustered—your brain is not available for future planning. When your nervous system is in the middle of an emotional storm, your best course of action is to simply wait until you calm down. Take a breath; take a walk; watch a brief video; eat a cookie. I'm serious. One of my clinical supervisors used to say, "You'd be surprised how often a cookie and some milk can save a situation." Just like you cannot reason with a toddler until the tantrum has subsided, you cannot reason with an emotionally triggered adult until the storm has subsided. It's simply not how the brain works.

When you're calm, find a quiet moment, grab your journal or a piece of paper and reflect on the following questions, which are divided into reflections about work and reflections about home. You can either reflect on all the questions or, if you're more pained by relationships in a specific environment, simply focus on that subset.

WORK

- How do I want to feel around *my* team? Do I feel this way? If not, what am I willing to change?

- What do I want *my* relationship with my clients to feel like? Do I feel this way? If not, what am I willing to change?

- If I think about my career one year from now, what memories do I want to have created in *my* career? What risks do *I* want to know I have taken for myself?

- If I imagine my teammates (or clients) talking about me when I wasn't around, what do *I* hope that they're saying about me? Right now, is it likely that they would be saying those things? Why or why not? What would I have to change now to increase the likelihood that they would feel this way about me in the future?

- If *I* had to work with me—if I became my own coworker— what would it be like? What would be good and what wouldn't?

- Do I care about *my* legacy as a leader? If so, how?

- If I imagined a major future moment in my career—a major promotion, a major product launch, my retirement celebration— how will *I* feel about the body of my work? What will I be most proud of? What regrets do I have?

HOME

- If I saw the story of my family turned into a movie, what would *I* like about the movie? What would pain me?

- If I were at the end of my life right now and I was reflecting back on my marriage as it currently stands, what am *I* most proud of? What regrets do I have?

- If I think about my romantic relationship one year from now, what memories do I want to have created in *my* relationship?

- If my children were to parent the way I parent, how would *I* feel about that?

- If my children were to bring home a spouse that acted a lot like me, how would *I* feel about that?

- If I think about my kids one year from now, what memories do I want to have created with them?

To see this process in action, consider Mia's story. Mia was suffering in her marriage. While she said there wasn't anything egregiously wrong with it, she felt sad, disconnected, and uninspired. For years, Mia tried to fix the marriage by complaining frequently to her husband, Liam. She complained that they weren't living a romantic life; she criticized the way he talked to her; she bemoaned that he didn't prioritize time with her.

Before Mia did this exercise, she saw Liam as the problem—the one who needed to change before she could access the relationship she wanted. In our work, Mia found the following question to be particularly energizing for her: "If I think about *my* relationship six months from now, what memories do I want to have created in my relationship?"

Mia started to understand the powerful reciprocity between her own emotional energy and relationship quality: the more she felt disappointed in her relationship, the more she criticized; the more she criticized, the more distant her relationship felt; the more distant her relationship felt, the more disappointed she felt. Mia started to see her power in her relationship not as some tired cliché but as a real force for change. She got clear on the things *she* wanted to feel, the lessons she wanted *her* children to witness, and the memories *she* wanted to make.

In particular, she realized she was especially disappointed that Liam had not taken initiative to create simple, romantic weekend memories she wanted. As she centered her own wanting, she decided to become a leader, instead of a passive participant, in her relationship. Mia's leadership showed up in simple but profound ways when she bought a new coffee machine, started buying pastries on Friday, and positioned two chairs to look out the window at their backyard. Liam willingly joined her for relaxed Saturday coffee and conversation.

Mia made other changes, too. She began speaking to Liam only in the way she wanted to be spoken to—her tone got softer and her messages more nurturing. It's important to note that, because she was very hurt by Liam, she was not making these changes for him, but for *herself and her kids*. As she led this energetic shift, she found herself genuinely more satisfied. She was enjoying her conversations with her husband more—both because she liked the conversation better and she felt more comfortable with her kids witnessing their increasingly respectful dialogue. She was particularly impressed when, as she started to recall her power in her marriage, Liam remembered his, too. Mia felt increasingly hopeful as Liam started to become more responsive in the ways she had been wanting, like when he bought tickets to a concert and planned a camping trip. By remembering *her* power in *her* relationship, Mia didn't just change herself, she changed the chemistry of her marriage and ultimately cocreated a more satisfying relationship.

This exercise produces exceptional change in workplace settings, too. For example, I've worked with leadership teams that struggle to connect with their teams or customers and fall into impotent blame traps. They start to endorse toothless beliefs, like "The problem with this team is no one's motivated!" or "The problem with my customers is everyone's too distracted." When they instead focus on what *they* want for *their* team or their business, they reactivate powerful agency. Here are some examples:

- A content creator, panicked by a lack of social media engagement, decides to stop obsessing about what types of content his audience wants and instead centers his own wanting. He asks himself, "If no one read this, liked this, or shared this, what could *I* write that would still light me up like a firecracker?" and then he writes that. Importantly, he realizes that the energetic line between performative production and authentic creation yields drastic improvements in his relationship with his audience—and it began with him centering his relationship with himself.

- An executive team, stressed about their team's lack of enthusiasm, strengthens their organization by determining, "What would *we* need to do to bring a new level of our own enthusiasm to this team?" As they start to clean up their own pain—their own conflicts and their own lack of inspiration—the organization changes: morale goes up, employee engagement scores rise, and job retention increases.

- A mother, frustrated by her tenuous relationship with her teenage daughter, improves her connection to her child by centering her own wanting. The mother doesn't want to overask, overcheck, or overanalyze her daughter's behavior, but thought she "had to." Turns out the daughter didn't want be on the receiving end of an energy the mother didn't want to give. What the mother really wanted was a relationship with her daughter that felt more relaxed, more trusting, and less demanding. As the mother started to do what *she* wanted, the relationship with her daughter improved. The mother was particularly amazed, one Friday evening around 8 p.m., when she unexpectantly asked her daughter, "What time are your friends coming to pick you up?" and her daughter responded, "They're not. You and I are watching a movie."

Whether you're thinking about your relationships at work or at home, if you want to create powerful relationships, there's one simple—and counterintuitive—thing you can do: Stop thinking about the other person and start thinking about your own emotional power.

When you start remembering your own power by acting like the leader, parent, coworker, and friend *you* want to be, you know who wins?

Everyone.

Don't Let Past Pain in Your Relationships Control Their Future Potential

Notice that there is generally a consistency to your relationships. Relationships have an energetic set point, a rhythm to which they naturally calibrate. Relationships that repeatedly disappoint you tend to persistently disappoint you; the ones that repeatedly enliven you continue to enliven you; the ones that bore you bore you; and so on. This is largely because your brain is a pattern detector, reflexively inserting past patterns over present interactions.

As we discussed in neuroenergetic code 2, the only way any pattern detector can work is if the past is superimposed on the present. The only reason you know "Apple" is the answer to a puzzle like this—Apple. Apple. Apple. [fill in the blank]—is because you have past data to insert in a future blank.

It's the way you *have felt* in your relationship that creates the energetic projection for how you *will feel* in your relationship. What I'm calling "energetic projections," you likely call memories. Memories are energetic imprints, the lingering neural sensations of how something affected you.[6]

While memories come in a variety of forms, neuroscientific evidence clearly demonstrates that emotional memories (as opposed to memories of facts) are most powerful.[7] Structures in your brain, like the amygdala and hippocampus—both of which are essential to your emotional memories—allow you to store and reactivate old memories to steer you through current relationships.

If the memories you've encoded about your relationship are generally positive, you will feel generally positive. If your memories are generally negative, you will feel generally negative. Regardless of how your relationships went in the past, this neuroenergetic code is designed to help you strengthen them for the future.

Exercise: Visualize It and Calibrate to It

To elevate the past patterning in your relationships, you need to engineer an expansive vision from the future. Do this through a two-step exercise:

1. Visualize it.

2. Calibrate to it.

Step 1: Visualize it

Research into visualization shows that for your visualization to be effective, you need to be highly specific with the images you imagine. Because it's difficult to create a vision of an entire relationship, all you'll need to do is simply visualize one clear "memory from the future." Identify the relationship you want to focus on and select a "target person." Your target person can be a specific individual, like a specific colleague, your partner, a client, your parent. Or the target person can be a group of people, like your team or your customers. All you will need is some paper and time for envisioning.

Also note, this is a great exercise to do with your team or your partner. People can complete it independently and then share their responses. It's powerful and unifying.

There are two steps to the visualization process.

1. Imagine a *specific, significant moment in the future* that will be deeply meaningful to your relationship with your target person. For example:

- If it's the first employee you've ever hired, you can envision your relationship at their one-year work anniversary.

- If you have a small startup, you can imagine you and your team's relationship when the company goes public.

- If it's your marriage, you can imagine a scene from the end of your life.

- If it's your young child, you can imagine the day they leave home for college or their wedding day.

2. Envision this scene playing out before you on a movie screen and focus intensely on *who you are in this scene*. This is not just any scene—it's an Oscar-worthy performance. This *is* a time for drama and details. You can see and feel everything about yourself: what you are saying, how you are feeling, how the people around you are feeling, your body language, their body language. Visualize intensely the way it all makes you feel. Now write it all out using as much detail as you can. Again, the science of visualization works most effectively when you are *highly* specific. Do not be bashful. This is private unless you choose to share it. Remember, lots of feeling and lots of detail.

Step 2: Calibrate to it

Now that you have written a clear vision—literally a specific script—of how you desire your relationship to feel in the future, all that's left to do is calibrate your energy to it. The future self you described in your vision is an energetic expansion of the leader you are right now. In other words, the version in your visualization is you but *more*. While I don't know what you wrote, I'm sure you described a more expansive version of yourself—maybe more confident, maybe more connected, peaceful, creative, or forgiving. Regardless of what you wrote, you described a more powerful version of yourself. In other words, at this exact moment, you are not calibrated to the vision you described. If you were already energetically able to hold your vision, it wouldn't occur to you to envision it because you would already have it.

For example, if you had a business that currently did $1 million in revenue per year and I asked you to envision a more expansive financial future for your business, you wouldn't say $1 million. You would project more—maybe $5 million, maybe $500 million. Whatever you project, you do not hold the energy for it right now. You'd have to evolve from where you are right now—your thinking, decision-making, and emotion regulation would all have to change to meet that future version of yourself. That's the point of the calibration.

Return to your visualization and ask yourself the following question: What is one specific, manageable, and clear thing I would be willing to do *no matter what* in order to evolve into the version of myself that has a stronger relationship with my target person?

Examples include:

- Stop criticizing my target person.

- Stop interrupting.

- Stop teasing.

- Give your target person one clear compliment each day. Say something so bold that it pushes you to your emotional edge (e.g., instead of quickly saying "nice presentation," look them square in the eye and say, "I wanted to make a point to tell you that I was really impressed by your presentation because [fill in the blank]).

- Offer your target person a thoughtful gesture every day, week, or month (e.g., buy them a cup of coffee; ask if you can get them anything from the cafeteria; send them a funny meme; ask them to go on a five-minute walk with you).

- Stop asking certain questions (e.g., "Why do you keep doing it like that?" or "When are you going to do that?").

- Start asking your target person a specific, predetermined question every time you see them (e.g., "What's new with you today?" or "Anything I can help you with?").

- Pray or do heart-centered meditations about this person every day, week, or month.

- Start devoting two minutes of non-work-related conversation with this person each day.

- Every time you interact with your target person learn something new about them. Note this in your phone and then make it a point to reference your knowledge of them in future conversations with them.

- Stop making rude gestures like sighs or eye rolls.

- Specifically create space for your target person to offer their opinion (e.g., "I've given my opinion but am genuinely interested in yours. What do you think about x?").

- Refuse to get into *any* conversations about who's right.

- Always take a deep breath before you speak to your target person regardless of the situation.

- Always remind yourself to soften your face and look your target person in the eye.

- Write a gratitude letter to your target person every day, week, or month, even if you never share it with the person.

The "no matter what" aspect of this exercise is highly powerful. If you can nail this aspect, your emotional power will skyrocket and your relationships will reap tremendous reward. When things are calm, it's easy to assume the relationship will be fine. For example, if you decided that it will be powerful for you to always take a deep breath before you speak to your target person, it's easy to see it as unnecessary when you find yourself having an easy conversation with your target person. It may seem unnecessary—awkward even—to always take a deep breath. Do it anyway. You are training yourself for elite levels of interpersonal energy. Hold your position. Practice.

The "no matter what" clause is even more important for the times you get triggered. When triggered, the allure of falling back into destructive relational patterns is extremely powerful. For example, imagine you decide that you will "stop being critical" in your romantic relationship, but then your partner starts loading the washing machine like some kind of savage and, gosh darn it, you just need this one exception. Real quick, you just need to tell your partner why that's the wrong way to do it. And also, why would they even think that's a good way to do it and, here, you know what, why don't you just get out of the way, and I'll do everything—because I'm ALWAYS THE ONE WHO DOES EVERYTHING AROUND HERE.

And, well, I'm sure you know the drill.

Calibrate up; hold your position *no matter what.*

I'll offer one final example that highlights the power of this code. Grace was a high-energy mother of two young children and an executive in a busy organization. Herself an only child, Grace was often deeply moved, thinking about the relationship her two daughters would form over their lifetime. In addition to being a bright, busy woman, Grace also had a great sense of humor. While she prided herself on her humor, she was very aware that her humor often had a biting, sarcastic edge.

One day, when her four-year-old daughter knocked over a tower she was building with her six-year-old sister, she heard her six-year-old say to her four-year-old, "You got rocks for hands? Don't be such a knucklehead!" The four-year-old burst into tears and the six-year-old retorted, "Relax; it's just a joke." Witnessing this interaction between her kids, Grace stiffened. Although Grace didn't go around calling people "knuckleheads," she clearly saw her own energetic thumbprint on this brusque interaction between her two young kids. Grace knew she was the one who taught her kids how to minimize other's injuries and call it funny. She realized that comments like those didn't invite connection; they rejected it.

As Grace envisioned her family's future relationship, she knew that she wanted to lead them on a softer, more connected path. She vowed that if she brought the energy into her home, she could lead it out. She started to envision how she wanted her family to interact in the future, and she realized that releasing her own sarcasm was a specific, manageable, and clear thing she would do to calibrate into a better version of herself. Although it still pains her every now and then when she has to let a good biting quip go by, she remains calibrated to her vision of softer, more tender relationships.

Evidence of the profound shift she initiated in her family came about three months later when her girls were again playing with blocks and the four-year-old again accidentally knocked over the tower they were building. As the four-year-old started to cry, the six-year-old said, "Don't cry, sister. We can just build it again." In this moment, Grace knew that the energy in her home had shifted and that she was leading her family toward a more rewarding future.

This raises a final point. When I do this exercise with people, some will ask me: How long do I need to hold this energetic standard? The answer is for as long as you think it's helpful to the degree you think it's helpful. In Grace's case, she decided she will no longer use sarcasm in certain relationships because the underlying energy doesn't align with the leadership she wants to embody. If, however, you choose something like always taking one breath or having a two-minute check-in per day with your target person, you should continue until the relationship reaches a point that you feel you've confidently achieved your new standard.

· · ·

One of the most profound ways to strengthen your relationships is to remember what relationships are: a *cocreation* between you and the people to whom you are connected. By virtue of your relationships being a direct product of *your* energy, you have tremendous agency in building the powerful, satisfying relationships you desire. How you harness your energy has much to do with what your relationships will become. Recognizing that relationships are energetic entities shifting in the tides of time highlights the importance of visualizing where you want to steer your relationships. Visualization, a form of neural conditioning, is the brain's portal that allows you to expand beyond the patterns of right now and arrive at a brighter promise of what could be.

Conclusion: Rising to Power

n order to do the work I do, I hold tight to the promise of a non-dualistic life—the idea that even in the dark, the light still shines. I have witnessed, time and time again, that it's in our moments of painful descent where we realize hope remains, strength persists, and connection endures.

It's in the falling that we see: Energy rises.

To access the full potential of your emotional power, you must learn to work with your emotional pain for one simple reason: Your most enduring pain comes from what you *already* think about yourself—that you're not good enough, important enough, or worthy enough. And the thing about this pain is that you can never outrun what *you* believe about yourself.

Through many years of working with all kinds of human heart-break, I've come to know there's a sacred promise in pain. The promise is this: The very things you think are too broken, too inadequate, too ugly, and too humiliating about you are not here to sink you. They're here to set you free.

Sound impossible?

It's not.

Your very life is already the evidence of the impossible made possible. You are, quite literally, energy incarnate. Your brain is an electrical machine that originated in the belly of stars approximately 13 billion years ago.[1] In my favorite quote describing the majesty of the brain, neuroscientist V. S. Ramachandran writes,

"How can a three-pound mass of jelly that you can hold in your palm imagine angels, contemplate the meaning of infinity, and even question its own place in the cosmos? Especially awe inspiring is the fact that any single brain, including yours, is made up of atoms that were forged in the hearts of countless, far-flung stars billions of years ago. These particles drifted for eons and light-years until gravity and change brought them together here, now. These atoms now form a conglomerate—your brain—that can not only ponder the very stars that gave it birth but can also think about its own ability to think and wonder about its own ability to wonder. With the arrival of humans, it has been said, the universe has suddenly become conscious of itself. This, truly, is the greatest mystery of all."[2]

For the tiniest sliver of time, about 700,000 hours, you are called forth into the pure potentiality of your own life. Your leadership—your energy to affect your life and the lives of those who depend on you—is your greatest power in this life. Whether your leadership is mediocre or masterful depends deeply on you. Often, when you lose your way, it's simply because you've forgotten what you *already* are.

You read this book because it was time to remember.

Tell me: In a life where you—through not an ounce of your own volition—energized a human body to live a human experience atop a strange ball floating through a dark universe that astrophysicists now believe is endless, what has happened to you that cannot be redeemed?[3]

What can't you have?

You want to change the way you show up in your life? Of course you can. You want to start a business? Of course you can. You want to lead your relationships with a degree of courage that takes your breath away? Of course you can. Heal your own trauma? Stop giving away your power for the booby prize of other people's approval? Slow the raging wave of intergenerational trauma for your children?

Of course you can.

Right now, more than anything else, the world needs leaders who believe in the *full* promise of our *full* humanity. Right now, the fate of so much—our relationships to each other, the safety of our children, and the viability of our planet—hangs in uncertainty's precarious balance. Human pain ignites in the energy of uncertainty. Everywhere you look, you'll see people who are in pain—on edge, suspicious, fearful, and exhausted. The world is waiting for people who aren't just aware of painful emotions, but ones who know precisely what to do about them.

The world is waiting for you.

And your most powerful service to the world doesn't require anything more than everything you already are. The world needs the full range of your energy. The world needs you to show them what to do with their fear, their rage, their inadequacy, their anxiety by watching you transform your own.

If there's one message I hope you carry with you from the collection of these codes, it's this: To lead powerfully, you must lead wholly. It's when you realize that you are on this planet to embody the whole energy of your whole life that you rise toward the only thing you ever wanted anyway: yourself. And in these moments, as you rise to claim the most powerful version of yourself, you show everyone else the way home, too.

Connecting the Codes: A Summary

Each neuroenergetic code offers powerful insights for strengthening your emotional power—your ability to stay strong in the midst of life's inevitable challenges. The neuroenergetic codes provide insight into the science behind how your brain works. When you more clearly understand how your brain constructs your reality, you can engineer your life in more satisfying and empowered ways. While profound on their own, the codes are most powerful when they're connected, collectively integrated and applied to your life. Below is a comprehensive summary of all eight codes.

Code 1: Expand Your Emotional Power

You expand your emotional power when you transform the energy trapped in your pain. This code shows you how to *expand your edge of emotional power* by using your emotional pain to strengthen your emotional power. To expand *your edge of emotional power*:

- **Pick a more powerful pain:** This strategy, with an accompanying four-part exercise, increases your emotional power by showing you how to stop pointlessly trying to eradicate your problems and instead start upgrading them.

- **Hold your emotional shake:** This strategy, with an accompanying two-part exercise, shows you how to hold more energy in your nervous system so you can become more emotionally powerful.

HIGHLIGHTS:

- Emotional pain is an energy.

- Because it's an energy, emotional pain is governed by the laws of physics, which tell us it can never be destroyed but it can be transformed.

- A significant amount of pain in your life is created when you repeatedly self-betray when you divide the truths of your emotions from the reality of your actions.

- To turn your pain into your power, stop working against what you really want.

- You cannot erase or eliminate your pain, but you can use its energy to fuel your emotional expansion.

- If you don't harness the energy of pain, it will suffocate you. If you do, it can empower you.

- When you expand the edge of your emotional power, the way you lead—at work and at home—becomes more effective.

Code 2: Build Your Power Pattern

A powerful feature of your brain is its pattern-detection abilities. Your patterns move you effortlessly through your life, but it's the quality of your patterns that determines whether you find yourself empowered or in pain. This code shows you how to build your power pattern. Through a three-step exercise—design it, test it, and repeat it—you learned how to create the boldest, bravest framework for your life, a framework that will allow you to lead powerfully in even the toughest moments of your life.

HIGHLIGHTS:

- Patterns are vital to your leadership because of how your brain works.

- The pattern-detection abilities of your brain are invested in your survival. *Everything else* is secondary. The surest test of survivability is *familiarity*. If you have been here before—no matter how bad you felt—it's familiar enough that your brain is certain you can survive it.

- Your leadership becomes more powerful when you look for patterns—not in your situations—but in your (often unconscious) emotional energy.

- Attempts to change patterns in your life fail when they overemphasize the situation. To change your patterns, you must tackle them at the level of *time* and *emotion*—examining how past feelings are informing your present situations.

Code 3: Harness Your Emotional Energetics

This code introduces you to the pain tree and shows you how to work with the singularly painful emotion of humiliation. Through the pain tree, you gained emotional clarity as you learned that many problems are caused by an (often unconscious) fear of humiliation, including problems that often appear to have nothing to do with humiliation. Two strategies, called releasing them and choosing you, showed you how to harness the energy of humiliation and become more emotionally powerful.

HIGHLIGHTS:

- No situation has meaning until it's electrified by your emotions.

- Many of the problems in your life are caused by an (often unconscious) avoidance of humiliation or potential humiliation.

- The emotional opposite of humiliation is worthiness.

- The energy of humiliation is so powerful that you see its profound effects across the range of human behavior, including employee engagement and combat veterans.

- Ostensibly harmless behaviors like exaggerating, venting, and gossiping hold the key to transforming your humiliation into empowerment.

Code 4: Master Uncertainty

Uncertainty has a predictable rhythm, a way it reliably makes you think and feel *regardless of situation*. You become much more emotionally powerful when you take your focus off solving every unresolved scenario and instead focus more on the person you *routinely* become in the shadow of uncertainty's energy. This code shows you how to master uncertainty by becoming the hero of your own story through two exercises:

- Be an information seeker, not a reassurance seeker: Reassurance seeking, the act of repeatedly looking for certain answers to unanswerable questions, weakens your emotional power. Information seeking strengthens it. This exercise helps you identify when you're information seeking versus when you're reassurance seeking.

- Say "I don't know": When you are uncertain, you only have two choices: You can pretend to know, or you can tell the truth. If you want to be the hero of your own story, find the power to say three brave words: "I don't know."

HIGHLIGHTS:
- Paradoxically, it's the things you do to avoid uncertainty—and not the uncertainty itself—that cause most of your emotional pain.

- All forms of anxiety—from the mild to the pathological—can be understood as a dysfunctional relationship with certainty.

- It's often the things you're doing to keep yourself safe from pain—overdoing, overworking, overgiving, overthinking—that are the cause of your pain, and not the uncertainty itself.

- There comes a point when the safety behaviors you're employing to stay safe from uncertainty become the very behaviors that injure you.

- It's only when you realize the true source of your pain that you can relieve it.

Code 5: Rewire Your Source Code

You strengthen the way you lead when you understand how you were led by your original leaders: your parents. Your parents provided you with your "source code," your earliest model of how leadership looks. This code allows you to improve internalized—and often unconscious—childhood "coding" that is currently blocking the full expression of your emotional power. By rewiring your source code, you no longer *react* to childhood triggers; instead, you *respond* from the unfiltered power of your emotional presence. You rewired your source code through a four-step process:

1. **Remember:** In this step, you remembered your source code by bringing unconscious material into your conscious awareness.

2. **Relate:** In this step, you related your earliest leadership experiences to the ways you currently lead your life at work and at home.

3. **Recognize:** In this step, you gained understanding of how your source code manifests in your life in ways you do not like.

4. **Rewire:** In this step, you rewired your source code by designing more emotionally powerful ways to lead your life.

HIGHLIGHTS:

- Because of the stunning brain development that occurs from birth to age five, much of your present-day leadership is related to patterns you learned in childhood.

- Your present-day overreactions (e.g., overthinking, overdoing, overworking) are related to childhood coding.

- By identifying experiences of your childhood pain—either ones you experienced directly *from* your parents or ones you witnessed *in* your parents—you will gain insight into how to strengthen your leadership today.

Code 6: Quit Commanding

Command energy is when you try to control other people's energy—their behaviors, thoughts, and feelings—so you don't have to exert energy to change your own. It's the energy of "you do what I say so I don't have to be different." This code shows you how to stop using command energy so you can build more powerful, dynamic, and interconnected relationships. Using a four-step process called "plug energetic leaks," you will no longer need to control other people, empowering you to show up as a stronger, calmer, and more confident leader.

HIGHLIGHTS:

- Command energy is extremely common in work, parenting, romantic relationships, and even on social media.

- In today's complex teams, families, and romances, command energy does not create deeply interconnected relationships because it blocks fairness and freedom.

- Commanding other people to behave in a way that aligns with your interests while denying theirs works against the fundamental design of their brain's drive for independence and erodes your influence in your relationships.

- This code shows you where you may be engaging in "energetic tugs-of-war," which are emotional standoffs that lessen your influence and weaken your relationships. This code also explains how to protect your relationships and strengthen your leadership by "dropping the rope."

Code 7: Unleash Your Magnetism

Magnetic leadership is when others follow you through the power of your example. This is the most powerful way to lead because it's the most aligned with how your brain operates. People are connected to you not because you *insist*, but because they *choose*—it's a neurological win-win. This code, through a series of reflections called "making magnetic relationships," shows you how to radiate a more magnetic energy in your leadership.

HIGHLIGHTS:

- People's universal and deepest desire is to be accepted for who they are—*to be worthy as they are.*

- When you stop obsessing about motivating others, you can focus on the only person you can control: yourself.

- When you powerfully lead yourself, people will follow because you become the evidence of the thing they want most in their lives: access to their own power.

Code 8: Build a Relationship from the Future

You create more powerful relationships at work and at home when you build a clear future vision of them. Relationships fall into pain largely because they are governed by past patterns that create repetition, stagnancy, and, in some cases, destruction. This code shows you how to create more powerful, energizing relationships with the people you care about—your clients, kids, colleagues, partner, or team—by building a future vision of those relationships. Having a clear vision of your future relationship allows you to:

- Remember your power as a cocreator in your relationship. By using a series of reflections, you recall your agency as a powerful cocreator in your relationships.

- Prevent past pain in your relationships from controlling their future potential. By using two strategies, you learn how to break out of stagnant relationship patterns by creating clear visions for your relationships and then calibrating your energy to them.

HIGHLIGHTS:

- Relationships are not stagnant; they are living, dynamic energetic entities that evolve through time.

- The science of visualization has a lot to offer your future relationships.

- Visualization isn't magic; it's neural conditioning.

- When you visualize your relationship in the future, you prime your nervous system to be in the optimal position to hold the emotional energy that you desire, particularly under emotionally challenging conditions.

- By centering your clear vision for the evolution of your relationships, you position yourself to be a powerful cocreator in your relationships instead of a passive participant.

NOTES

Introduction

1. Neuroscience has amassed an impressive arsenal of tools like fMRI, EEG, deep brain stimulation (DBS), and transcranial magnetic stimulation (TMS) that rely on the brain's energy. Functional magnetic resonance imaging measures chemical changes in the brain using oxygen metabolism. See Richard B. Buxton, "The Physics of Functional Magnetic Resonance Imaging (fMRI)," *Reports on Progress in Physics* 76, no. 9 (2013): 096601, doi: 10.1088/0034-4885/76/9/096601, Epub 2013 Sep 4, PMID: 24006360; PMCID: PMC4376284. EEG measures electrical activity of large, synchronously firing populations of neurons in the brain. See Gregory A. Light et al., "Electroencephalography (EEG) and Event-Related Potentials (ERPs) with Human Participants," *Current Protocols in Neuroscience* (July 2010), chapter 6: unit 6.25.1-24, doi: 10.1002/0471142301.ns0625s52, PMID: 20578033; PMCID: PMC2909037. While some tools are mostly used in research capacities, others have profound application to people's real lives. For example, deep brain stimulation (DBS) has delivered astounding improvements to people's lives by using a small device to regulate abnormal electrical activity in the brain. In deep brain stimulation (DBS), implanted electrodes deliver electricity to specific dysfunctional areas of the brain. See Andres M. Lozano et al., "Deep Brain Stimulation: Current Challenges and Future Directions," *Nature Reviews Neurology* 15, no. 3 (March 2019): 148–160, doi: 10.1038/s41582-018-0128-2, PMID: 30683913; PMCID: PMC6397644. Transcranial magnetic stimulation (TMS) can improve people's emotions by pulsing magnetic energy into the brain. This form of brain stimulation provokes excitation of neurons in certain brain areas. See Amit Chail, Rajiv Kumar Saini, P. S. Bhat, Kalpana Srivastava, and Vinay Chauhan, "Transcranial Magnetic Stimulation: A Review of Its Evolution and Current Applications," *Industrial Psychiatry Journal* 27, no. 2 (July–December 2018): 172–180, doi: 10.4103/ipj.ipj_88_18, PMID: 31359968; PMCID: PMC6592198. In terms of application, repetitive transcranial magnetic stimulation (rTMS) delivered to the left dorsolateral prefrontal cortex (DLPFC) is a noninvasive brain stimulation technique approved by FDA for treatment-resistant depression. For more, see Mark S. George, Joseph J. Taylor, and E. Baron Short, "The Expanding Evidence Base for rTMS Treatment of Depression," *Current Opinion in Psychiatry* 26, no. 1 (January 2013): 13–18, doi: 10.1097/YCO.0b013e32835ab46d, PMID: 23154644; PMCID: PMC4214363.

2. For more, see Charles C. H. Cohen et al., "Saltatory Conduction along Myelinated Axons Involves a Periaxonal Nanocircuit," *Cell* 180, no. 2 (January 2020): 311–322e15, doi: 10.1016/j.cell.2019.11.039, Epub 2019 Dec 26, PMID: 31883793; PMCID: PMC6978798; and J. B. Hursh, "Conduction Velocity and Diameter of Nerve Fibers," *American Journal of Physiology*, 127, no. 1 (July 1939): 131–139. National Institutes of Health (US) Biological Sciences Curriculum Study, "Information about the Brain," *NIH Curriculum Supplement Series [Internet]* (Bethesda, MD: National Institutes of Health [US], 2007), https://www.ncbi.nlm.nih.gov/books/NBK20367/.

3. For more, see Masaaki Tanaka, Sanae Fukuda, Kei Mizuno, Hirohiko Kuratsune, and Yasuyoshi Watanabe, "Stress and Coping Styles Are Associated with Severe Fatigue in Medical Students," *Behavioral Medicine* 35, no. 3 (Fall 2009): 87–92, doi: 10.1080/089642 80903231979, PMID: 19812026. See also: American Psychiatric Association, *Diagnostic and Statistical Manual of Mental Disorders*, 5th ed. (2013), https://doi.org/10.1176/appi.books.978089 0425596; D. H. Barlow, *Anxiety and Its Disorders: The Nature and Treatment of Anxiety and Panic*, 2nd ed. (New York: Guilford Press, 2002); and World Health Organization, *International Statistical Classification of Diseases and Related Health Problems*, 11th ed. (Geneva: World Health Organization, 2019), https://icd.who.int/.

4. For a more comprehensive description of my work, see www.drjuliadigangi.com.

5. For more, see Elaine Hatfield, John T. Cacioppo, and Richard Rapson, "Emotional Contagion," in *Studies in Emotion and Social Interaction* (Cambridge: Cambridge University Press, 1993), 10.1017/CBO9781139174138; Carolina Herrando and Efthymios Constantinides, "Emotional Contagion: A Brief Overview and Future Directions," *Frontiers in Psychology* 12 (July 2021): 712606, doi: 10.3389/fpsyg.2021.712606, PMID: 34335425; PMCID: PMC8322226; and Lauri Nummenmaa, Jussi Hirvonen, Riitta Parkkola, and Jari K. Hietanen, "Is Emotional Contagion Special? An fMRI Study on Neural Systems for Affective and Cognitive Empathy," *Neuroimage* 43, no. 3 (November 2008): 571–580, doi: 10.1016/j.neuroimage.2008.08.014, Epub 2008 Aug 26, PMID: 18790065.

Understanding Your Emotional Power

1. If you're interested in an even deeper dive into the intricacies of emotion research, consider this: converging evidence from both human and animal studies reliably elucidates specific circuits in your brain that ultimately give rise to your experiences of emotional pain. While in laboratory settings distinctions between constructs like stress, fear, and anxiety can occasionally be meaningful, even then each of these constructs still activate the frontolimbic circuit. All of this is to say, the parts of your brain that give rise to your bad feelings—the feelings I will call "emotional pain"—consistently arise from activations to this central "emotional pain processing highway." Also note that because these parts of the brain underpin a wide range of negative emotion, they activate across many situations in your life. For example, they activate when you run from a lion and when you don't respect your own boundaries. In these examples, when the lion jumps out at you, you feel fear, which then motivates your behavior to run. When you don't hold a boundary that *you* want to hold, you may fail to hold your boundary because you perceive some threat (e.g., someone will get mad at you) that makes you then feel something like anxiety, stress, or fear. However, in the case of the lion, your running achieved your ultimate desired outcome (i.e., you escaped from the lion and the situation ends). But when you routinely don't honor the choices you *want* to make, *you* ultimately create *more* pain for yourself. In other words, when you divide yourself from the truth of your own wanting, you feel *more* pain: more *irritation* with yourself, more *frustration* with others, more *fear* that you're not safe in your relationships, more *anger* that this keeps happening to you, and so on. Finally, it is important to note that these regions of the brain are so vital to your survival that they can activate even when you're not consciously aware of the process I'm describing here. For more, see Dan W. Grupe and Jack B. Nitschke, "Uncertainty and Anticipation in Anxiety: An Integrated Neurobiological and Psychological Perspective," *Nature Reviews Neuroscience* 14, no. 7 (July 2013): 488–501, doi: 10.1038/nrn3524, PMID: 23783199; PMCID: PMC4276319; Cyril Herry, et al., "Processing of Temporal Unpredictability in Human and Animal Amygdala," *Journal of Neuroscience* 27, no. 22 (May 2007): 5958–5966, https://www.jneurosci.org/content/27/22/5958; Lisa M. Shin and Israel Liberzon, "The

Neurocircuitry of Fear, Stress, and Anxiety Disorders," *Neuropsychopharmacology* 35, no. 1 (January 2010): 169–191, doi: 10.1038/npp.2009.83; Dean Mobbs, et al., "On the Nature of Fear: Experts from the Fields of Human and Animal Affective Neuroscience Discuss Their Own Definitions of Fear and How We Should Study It," *Nature Neuroscience*, October 10, 2019, https://www.scientificamerican.com/article/on-the-nature-of-fear/.

    2. For more, see Chai M. Tyng, Hafeez U. Amin, Mohamad M. N. Saad, and Aamir S. Malik, "The Influences of Emotion on Learning and Memory," *Frontiers in Psychology* 8 (August 2017): 1454, doi: 10.3389/fpsyg.2017.01454, PMID: 28883804; PMCID: PMC5573739; C. Daniel Salzman and Stefano Fusi, "Emotion, Cognition, and Mental State Representation in Amygdala and Prefrontal Cortex," *Annual Review of Neuroscience* 33 (2010): 173–202, doi: 10.1146/annurev.neuro.051508.135256, PMID: 20331363; PMCID: PMC3108339. Also see the paper by Duncan and Barrett in which they suggest emotion is not separate from thinking but itself a form of cognition. They demonstrate that the brain's affective (i.e., emotional) areas overlap in what have traditionally been considered the brain's "cognitive" areas. Given that affective circuits modulate sensory processing, affective processing is an integral component of sensory experience and not a separate cognitive function that is subsequently performed on sensations. They write, "As a result, affect is an intrinsic property in all psychological phenomena that result from so-called 'cognitive' processes (such as consciousness, language, and memory). Affect and cognition, then, are not ontologically separate, but they are, perhaps, phenomenologically distinct. This is distinction in experience, however, rather than a distinction that exists in the structure of the brain or the psychological processes that produce that experience." For more, see Seth Duncan and Lisa Feldman Barrett, "Affect Is a Form of Cognition: A Neurobiological Analysis," *Cognition and Emotion* 21, no. 6 (September 2007): 1184–1211, doi: 10.1080/02699930701437931, PMID: 18509504; PMCID: PMC2396787. Additionally, neuropsychological functions that have been historically viewed as cognitive, such as memory, are now understood to be inextricable from affective processes in the brain. Take memory, for example. You don't remember *objectively*; you remember *emotionally*. Your brain preferentially encodes both positive *and* negative emotional events as compared to non-emotional events. Roger Brown and James Kulik, "Flashbulb Memories," *Cognition* 5, no. 1 (1977): 73–99, https://doi.org/10.1016/0010-0277(77)90018-X. More-recent advances in neuroscience have shown that emotional memory is privileged because of how your amygdala reacts and subsequently communicates with other structures in your frontal and temporal lobes, like the prefrontal cortex and the hippocampus. See Mark P. Richardson, Bryan A. Strange, and Raymond J. Dolan, "Encoding of Emotional Memories Depends on Amygdala and Hippocampus and Their Interactions," *Nature Neuroscience* 7 (2004): 278–285, https://doi.org/10.1038/nn1190; Salzman and Fusi, "Emotion, Cognition, and Mental State Representation." McGaugh's memory modulation hypothesis proposes that the amygdala enhances memory for emotionally arousing events by recruiting adrenergic and cortisol stress-hormone systems that then interact to promote memory storage in the cortex. See James L. McGaugh, "The Amygdala Modulates the Consolidation of Memories of Emotionally Arousing Experiences," *Annual Review of Neuroscience* 27 (2004): 1–28, https://pubmed.ncbi.nlm.nih.gov/15217324/. Compelling evidence from human studies support this hypothesis. See Kevin S. LaBar and Roberto Cabeza, "Cognitive Neuroscience of Emotional Memory," *Nature Reviews Neuroscience* 7 (2006): 54–64, https://doi.org/10.1038/nrn1825. Also note: Although the amygdala is popularly associated with fear, it is now understood to play a broader role in learning processes. For more, see M. Baxter and E. A. Murray, "The Amygdala and Reward," *Nature Reviews Neuroscience* 3 (2002): 563–573; and David Sander, Jordan Grafman, and Tiziana Zalla, "The Human Amygdala: An Evolved System for Relevance Detection," *Reviews in the Neurosciences* 14, no. 4 (2003): 303–316, doi: 10.1515/revneuro.2003.14.4.303, PMID: 14640318.

3. Lisa Feldman Barrett, Batja Mesquita, Kevin N. Ochsner, and James J. Gross, "The Experience of Emotion," *Annual Review of Psychology* 58 (2007): 373–403, doi: 10.1146/annurev.psych.58.110405.085709, PMID: 17002554; PMCID: PMC1934613.

4. Post-traumatic growth is one powerful example of how working with negative emotional energy in the wake of extreme adversity can lead to greater emotional power (e.g., resilience, confidence). Post-traumatic growth describes enduring positive psychological change experienced as a result of adversity or trauma. For more, see Richard G. Tedeschi and Lawrence G. Calhoun, "Posttraumatic Growth: Conceptual Foundations and Empirical Evidence," *Psychological Inquiry* 15, no. 1 (2004): 1–18, doi: 10.1207/s15327965pli1501_01; and Xiaoli Wu et al., "The Prevalence of Moderate-to-High Posttraumatic Growth: A Systematic Review and Meta-Analysis," *Journal of Affective Disorders* 243 (January 2019): 408–415, doi: 10.1016/j.jad.2018.09.023, Epub 2018 Sep 12, PMID: 30268956. Much of my own work in cognitive and affective neuroscience draws on cognitive reappraisal, a neurologically well-studied phenomenon that illustrates how the brain transforms emotional experiences. Extensive amounts of neuropsychological and behavioral evidence demonstrates that no event has a set emotional meaning. People can have widely varied emotional responses to identical stimuli. In broad terms, neural correlates of reappraisal include increased activation in lateral and medial prefrontal regions decreased activation of the amygdala and medial orbito-frontal cortex. For more, see K. N. Ochsner, S. A. Bunge, J. J. Gross, and J. D. Gabrieli, "Rethinking Feelings: An FMRI Study of the Cognitive Regulation of Emotion," *Journal of Cognitive Neuroscience* 8, no. 14 (November 2002): 1215–1229, doi: 10.1162/089892902760807212, PMID: 12495527.

5. Cortical midline structures (CMS), which include the posterior cingulate cortex, precuneus, anterior cingulate cortex, and various prefrontal areas, are thought to be responsible for self-referential processing. Meta-analytic results by Northoff et al. shows that self-referential processing is mediated by cortical midline structures. See Georg Northoff et al., "Self-Referential Processing in Our Brain—A Meta-Analysis of Imaging Studies on the Self," *NeuroImage* 31, no. 1 (2006): 440–457.

6. For more on how CMS are related to emotional power (e.g., self-esteem, self-confidence, self-assuredness), see Charlotte C. van Schie, Chui-De Chiu, Serge A. R. B. Rombouts, Willem J. Heiser, and Bernet M. Elzinga, "When Compliments Do Not Hit but Critiques Do: An fMRI Study into Self-Esteem and Self-Knowledge in Processing Social Feedback," *Social Cognitive and Affective Neuroscience* 13, no. 4 (April 2018): 404–417, doi: 10.1093/scan/nsy014, PMID: 29490088; PMCID: PMC5928412. See also Elizabeth F. Chua, Daniel L. Schacter, Erin Rand-Giovannetti, and Reisa A. Sperling, "Understanding Metamemory: Neural Correlates of the Cognitive Process and Subjective Level of Confidence in Recognition Memory," *Neuroimage* 29, no. 4 (February 2006): 1150–1160, doi: 10.1016/j.neuroimage.2005.09.058, Epub 2005 Nov 21, PMID: 16303318. See also Jacqueline Lutz et al., "Neural Activations during Self-Related Processing in Patients with Chronic Pain and Effects of a Brief Self-Compassion Training—A Pilot Study," *Psychiatry Research: Neuroimaging* 304 (October 2020): 111–155, doi: 10.1016/j.pscychresns.2020.111155, Epub 2020 Jul 30, PMID: 32799058; PMCID: PMC8100920.

Code 1: Expand Your Emotional Power

1. Exposure therapy is an evidence-based treatment predicated on people approaching situations in their life to provoke feelings that they have been avoiding (e.g., fear, anxiety, stress). Research shows that exposure therapy is a helpful treatment—often the most evidence-based treatment—for a range of problems such as OCD, PTSD, generalized

anxiety, phobias, social anxiety, and panic. See, for example, Cloe Ferrando and Caroline Selai, "A Systematic Review and Meta-Analysis on the Effectiveness of Exposure and Response Prevention Therapy in the Treatment of Obsessive-Compulsive Disorder," *Journal of Obsessive-Compulsive and Related Disorders* 31 (2021): 100684, 10.1016/j.jocrd.2021.100684. For more, see Carmen P. McLean, Hannah C. Levy, Madeleine L. Miller, and David F. Tolin, "Exposure Therapy for PTSD: A Meta-Analysis," *Clinical Psychology Review* 91, no. 3 (December 2021): 102115, doi: 10.1016/j.cpr.2021.102115, Epub 2021 Dec 21, PMID: 34954460; and Laura E. Watkins, Kelsey R. Sprang, and Barbara O. Rothbaum, "Treating PTSD: A Review of Evidence-Based Psychotherapy Interventions," *Frontiers in Behavioral Neuroscience* 12 (2018): 258, doi: 10.3389/fnbeh.2018.00258, PMID: 30450043; PMCID: PMC6224348.

2. See, for example, B. S. McEwen and R. M. Sapolsky, "Stress and Cognitive Function," *Current Opinion in Neurobiology* 5, no. 2 (April 1995): 205–216, doi: 10.1016/0959-4388(95)80028-x, PMID: 7620309; Christoph Radenbach et al., "The Interaction of Acute and Chronic Stress Impairs Model-Based Behavioral Control," *Psychoneuroendocrinology* 53 (March 2015): 268–280, doi: 10.1016/j.psyneuen.2014.12.017, Epub 2015 Jan 7, PMID: 25662093; Tom C. Russ et al., "Association between Psychological Distress and Mortality: Individual Participant Pooled Analysis of 10 Prospective Cohort Studies," *BMJ* 345 (2012): e4933, doi:10.1136/bmj.e4933; and Holly H. Schiffrin and S. Katherine Nelson, "Stressed and Happy? Investigating the Relationship between Happiness and Perceived Stress," *Journal of Happiness Studies* 11 (2010): 33–39, https://doi.org/10.1007/s10902-008-9104-7.

3. For more, see Angela D. Friederici, "The Brain Basis of Language Processing: From Structure to Function," *Physiological Reviews* 91, no. 4 (2011): 1357–1392, doi: 10.1152/physrev.00006.2011, PMID: 22013214; A. R. Hariri, S. Y. Bookheimer, and J. C. Mazziotta, "Modulating Emotional Responses: Effects of a Neocortical Network on the Limbic System," *Neuroreport* 11, no. 1 (January 2000): 43–48, doi: 10.1097/00001756-200001170-00009, PMID: 10683827; and Matthew D. Lieberman et al., "Putting Feelings into Words: Affect Labeling Disrupts Amygdala Activity in Response to Affective Stimuli," *Psychological Science* 18, no. 5 (May 2007): 421–428, doi: 10.1111/j.1467-9280.2007.01916.x, PMID: 17576282. Note also that language is a complex phenomenon involving both cortical and subcortical regions of the brain. However, language—specifically comprehension and production—is generally considered to be a cortical function.

4. For more, see Jessica L. Maples-Keller and Sheila A. M. Rauch, "Habituation," in J. S. Abramowitz and S. M. Blakey, eds., *Clinical Handbook of Fear and Anxiety: Maintenance Processes and Treatment Mechanisms*, 249–263 (Washington, DC: American Psychological Association, 2020), https://doi.org/10.1037/0000150-014.

Code 2: Build Your Power Pattern

1. The brain's pattern detection—or predictive processing—abilities have long been recognized by psychologists and neuroscientists. The benefits of prediction have been recognized across a variety of domains including motor, perceptual, behavioral, emotional, relational, and more. Superior pattern processing (SPP) abilities of the brain have been suggested as the foundational basis of the uniqueness of the human brain, allowing for theory of mind, language, humor, creativity, invention, inference, and more. The pattern processing abilities of the brain rely on broad neural networks. For more on the brain's pattern-detection abilities, see Mark P. Mattson, "Superior Pattern Processing Is the Essence of the Evolved Human Brain," *Frontiers in Neuroscience* 8 (August 2014): 265, doi: 10.3389/fnins.2014.00265, PMID: 25202234; PMCID: PMC4141622.

2. Andreja Bubic, D. Yves von Cramon, and Ricarda I. Schubotz, "Prediction, Cognition and the Brain," *Frontiers in Human Neuroscience* 4 (March 2010): 25, doi: 10.3389 /fnhum.2010.00025, PMID: 20631856; PMCID: PMC2904053.

3. See, for example, Julia A. DiGangi et al., "Differential Impact of Post-Deployment Stress and PTSD on Neural Reactivity to Emotional Stimuli in Iraq and Afghanistan Veterans," *Journal of Psychiatric Research* 96 (January 2018): 9–14, https://dolcoslab.beckman .illinois.edu/sites/default/files/DiGangi_etal_2017InPress_JPsychatrResearch_Post -deploymentStress-PTSD-ERP.pdf; and Julia A. DiGangi et al., "An Electrocortical Investigation of Emotional Face Processing in Military-Related Posttraumatic Stress Disorder," *Journal of Psychiatric Research* 92 (September 2017): 132–138, doi: 10.1016/j.jpsychires.2017.03.013.

4. See, for example, Rebecca E. Cooney, Lauren Y. Atlas, Jutta Joormann, Fanny Eugène, and Ian H. Gotlib, "Amygdala Activation in the Processing of Neutral Faces in Social Anxiety Disorder: Is Neutral Really Neutral?," *Psychiatry Research: Neuroimaging* 148, no. 1 (November 2006): 55–59, doi: 10.1016/j.pscychresns.2006.05.003, Epub 2006 Oct 9, PMID: 17030117.

5. Lisa Feldman Barrett, "You Aren't at the Mercy of Your Emotions—Your Brain Creates Them," TED talk, YouTube, January 2018, https://www.technologynetworks.com /neuroscience/videos/you-arent-at-the-mercy-of-your-emotions-your-brain-creates-them -298661.

6. For more, see Julia A. DiGangi et al., "Pretrauma Risk Factors for Posttraumatic Stress Disorder: A Systematic Review of the Literature," *Clinical Psychology Review* 33, no. 6 (August 2013): 728–744, doi: 10.1016/j.cpr.2013.05.002, Epub 2013 May 14, PMID: 23792469.

7. For more, see Eberhard Fuchs and Gabriele Flügge, "Adult Neuroplasticity: More Than 40 Years of Research," *Neural Plasticity* (2014): 541870, doi: 10.1155/2014/541870, Epub 2014 May 4, PMID: 24883212; PMCID: PMC402697.

8. See Harold Evans, "Einstein's 2,998 Mistakes," *Los Angeles Times*, November 1, 2004, https://www.latimes.com/archives/la-xpm-2004-nov-01-oe-evans1-story.html.

Code 3: Harness Your Emotional Energetics

1. Grief can be such a searingly painful emotion that it deserves its own mention. The energy of grief may seem, on its face, vastly different than the energy of humiliation. But grief—along with other related and deeply painful emotions like loneliness or abandonment—is still integrally linked to our sense of worthiness and wholeness. The experience of grief creates a profound sense of aloneness. It's the sensation that something inextricably vital to our personal wholeness (e.g., a spouse, an identity) has been taken. Even when we know it's not rational, we can feel like we have been abandoned and, in this experience, we feel deeply alone. After being stripped of something so vital, many people naturally start to question the value of their own life in ways that can lead to painful existential questions, such as "What good is my life now?" or "How could I matter so little to God that the things that mattered most have been taken from me?" As with the energy of humiliation, when working with the energy of grief, it's essential to address core issues of emotional power— the idea that worth is *unconditional*. Emotional power is the idea that even in the most difficult situations we still possess value and strength. Psychiatrist and grief expert Colin Murray Parkes writes that the most important thing healthcare professionals "have to offer (the grieving) is our confidence in their personal worth and strength." For more, see Colin Murray Parkes, "Bereavement in Adult Life," *BMJ* 316 (March 1998): 856–859, doi: 10.1136 /bmj.316.7134.856, PMID: 9549464; PMCID: PMC1112778.

2. For more, see Paul Fairlie, "Meaningful Work, Employee Engagement, and Other Key Employee Outcomes: Implications for Human Resource Development," *Advances in Developing Human Resources* 13, no. 4 (2011): 508–525, https://doi.org/10.1177/152342231 1431679.

3. Sarah F. Brosnan, "Nonhuman Species' Reactions to Inequity and Their Implications for Fairness," *Social Justice Research* 19, no. 2 (2006): 153–185, https://psycnet.apa.org /record/2006-11512-001.

Code 4: Master Uncertainty

1. For more, see Archy O. de Berker et al., "Computations of Uncertainty Mediate Acute Stress Responses in Humans," *Nature Communications* 7 (March 2016): 10996, https://doi.org/10.1038/ncomms10996.

2. For more, see R. Nicholas Carleton et al., "Increasingly Certain about Uncertainty: Intolerance of Uncertainty across Anxiety and Depression," *Journal of Anxiety Disorders* 26, no. 3 (April 2012) : 468–479, doi: 10.1016/j.janxdis.2012.01.011, Epub Feb 7, 2012, PMID: 22366534; and Dan W. Grupe and Jack B. Nitschke, "Uncertainty and Anticipation in Anxiety: An Integrated Neurobiological and Psychological Perspective," *Nature Reviews Neuroscience* 14, no. 7 (July 2013): 488–501, doi: 10.1038/nrn3524, PMID: 23783199; PMCID: PMC4276319.

3. Earlier thought to be a fear-based disorder, PTSD is now understood to involve broad aberrations in both cognitive and affective processes. For example, PTSD is now thought to involve disruptions to learning and memory that affect processing of context (i.e., what is safe context vs. what is a dangerous context). Exaggerated fear and sustained distress are thought to be due, not entirely to the trauma itself, but to a broader failure of emotional responses to extinguish in the absence of threat. Research shows that people with PTSD exhibit lower activations in brain regions promoting safety signal processing, such as the ventromedial prefrontal cortex (vmPFC) and hippocampus. For more, see Mohammed R. Milad, Roger K. Pitman, Cameron B. Ellis, Andrea L. Gold, Lisa M. Shin, Natasha B. Lasko, Mohamed A. Zeidan, Kathryn Handwerger, Scott P. Orr, and Scott L. Rauch, "Neurobiological Basis of Failure to Recall Extinction Memory in Posttraumatic Stress Disorder," *Biological Psychiatry* 66, no. 12 (December 2009): 1075–1082, doi: 10.1016/j .biopsych.2009.06.026, Epub Sept. 12, 2009, PMID: 19748076; PMCID: PMC2787650.

4. For more, see Hugo D. Critchley, Christopher J. Mathias, and Raymond J. Dolan, "Neural Activity in the Human Brain Relating to Uncertainty and Arousal during Anticipation," *Neuron* 29, no. 2 (February 2001): 537–545, 10.1016/S0896-6273(01)00225-2.

Code 5: Rewire Your Source Code

1. Thomas R. Insel and Larry J. Young, "The Neurobiology of Attachment," *Nature Reviews Neuroscience* 2, no. 2 (February 2001): 129–136, doi: 10.1038/35053579, PMID: 11252992. For more see, J. Bowlby, *Attachment and Loss, Vol. 1* (New York: Basic Books, 1969); Mary D. Salter Ainsworth, Mary C. Bleha, Everett Waters, and Sally N. Wall, *Patterns of Attachment* (Hillsdale, NJ: Erlbaum, 1978); K. Lorenz, "Der Kumpan in der Umwelt des Vogels," *Journal für Ornithologie* 83: 289–413; L. A. Sroufe, E. A. Carlson, A. K. Levy et al., "Implications of Attachment Theory for Developmental Psychopathology," *Development and Psychopathology* 11 (1999): 1–13; and M. Noriuchi, Y. Kikuchi, and A. Senoo, "The Functional Neuroanatomy of Maternal Love: Mother's Response to Infant's Attachment Behaviors," *Biological Psychiatry* 63 (2008): 415–423.

2. See "InBrief: The Science of Early Childhood Development," Center on the Developing Child, Harvard, www.developingchild.harvard.edu; and Lise Eliot, *What's Going On in There?* (New York: Bantam, 2010). For more on the profound development that happens in childhood brain development, see also Joan Stiles and Terry L. Jernigan, "The Basics of Brain Development," *Neuropsychology Review* 20, no. 4 (December 2010): 327–348, doi: 10.1007/s11065-010-9148-4, Epub 2010 Nov 3, PMID: 21042938; PMCID: PMC2989000.

3. Marcus Quirin, Omri Gillath, Jens C. Pruessner, and Lucas D. Eggert, "Adult Attachment Insecurity and Hippocampal Cell Density," *Social Cognitive and Affective Neuroscience* 5, no. 1 (March 2010): 39–47, doi: 10.1093/scan/nsp042, Epub 2009 Dec 9, PMID: 20007241; PMCID: PMC2840841; and Robin A. Barry, Grazyna Kochanska, and Robert A. Philibert, "G x E Interaction in the Organization of Attachment: Mothers' Responsiveness as a Moderator of Children's Genotypes," *Journal of Child Psychology and Psychiatry* 49, no. 12 (December 2008): 1313–1320, doi: 10.1111/j.1469-7610.2008.01935.x, PMID: 19120710; PMCID: PMC2688730.

4. For more, see Morris Moscovitch et al., "Functional Neuroanatomy of Remote Episodic, Semantic and Spatial Memory: A Unified Account Based on Multiple Trace Theory," *Journal of Anatomy* 207, no. 1 (July 2005): 35–66, doi: 10.1111/j.1469-7580 .2005.00421.x, PMID: 16011544; PMCID: PMC1571502.

5. Larry R. Squire and Adam J. O. Dede, "Conscious and Unconscious Memory Systems," *Cold Spring Harbor Perspectives in Biology* 7, no. 3 (March 2015): a021667. doi: 10.1101/cshperspect.a021667, PMID: 25731765; PMCID: PMC4355270.

6. Patricia J. Bauer, *Remembering the Times of Our Lives* (Mahwah, NJ: Lawrence Erlbaum Associates, 2007); and Patricia J. Bauer, "The Development of Forgetting: Childhood Amnesia" in Patricia J. Bauer and Robyn Fivush, eds., *The Wiley-Blackwell Handbook on the Development of Children's Memory*, vol. 2 (West Sussex, UK: Wiley-Blackwell, 2014). There are many component parts that describe what researchers call "childhood amnesia." In broad terms, it is thought that children are able to retrieve autobiographical memories once they develop autonoetic consciousness, the awareness of themselves as entities moving through time. Once children develop this ability, typically around age seven, autobiographical recall increases dramatically.

7. Micha Popper, Ofra Mayseless, and Omri Castelnovo, "Transformational Leadership and Attachment," *The Leadership Quarterly* 11, no. 2 (June 2000): 267–289, https://doi.org/10 .1016/S1048-9843(00)00038-2; Han Ik Yoo, Boong-Nyun Kim, Min Sup Shin, Soo Churl Cho, and Kang-E Hong, "Parental Attachment and Its Impact on the Development of Psychiatric Manifestations in School-Aged Children," *Psychopathology* 39, no. 4 (2006): 165–174; and Joan S. Tucker and Sherry L. Anders, "Attachment Style, Interpersonal Perception Accuracy, and Relationship Satisfaction in Dating Couples," *Personality and Social Psychology Bulletin* 25, no. 4 (1999): 403–412.

8. Karin Roelofs, "Freeze for Action: Neurobiological Mechanisms in Animal and Human Freezing," *Philosophical Transactions of the Royal Society B* 372, no. 1718 (April 2017): 20160206, doi: 10.1098/rstb.2016.0206, PMID: 28242739; PMCID: PMC5332864.

9. Michael S. Fanselow, "Neural Organization of the Defensive Behavior System Responsible for Fear," *Psychonomic Bulletin and Review* 1, no. 4 (December 1994): 429–438, doi: 10.3758/BF03210947, PMID: 24203551.

10. Chris Cantor and John Price, "Traumatic Entrapment, Appeasement and Complex Post-Traumatic Stress Disorder: Evolutionary Perspectives of Hostage Reactions, Domestic Abuse and the Stockholm Syndrome," *Australian and New Zealand Journal of Psychiatry* 41, no. 5 (May 2007): 377–384, doi: 10.1080/00048670701261178, PMID: 17464728.

Connect to Others

1. Thomas R. Insel and Larry J. Young, "The Neurobiology of Attachment," *Nature Reviews Neuroscience* 2, no. 2 (February 2001): 129–136, doi: 10.1038/35053579, PMID: 11252992.

2. Interpersonal neurobiology is formally defined as human development that occurs within a social world in transaction with the functions of the brain that give rise to the mind. For more, see Daniel J. Siegel, "Toward an Interpersonal Neurobiology of the Developing Mind: Attachment Relationships, 'Mindsight,' and Neural Integration," *Infant Mental Health Journal* 22, no. 1–2 (2001): 67–94, https://doi.org/10.1002/1097-0355(200101 /04)22:1<67::AID-IMHJ3>3.0.CO;2-G.

Code 7: Unleash Your Magnetism

1. Ron Friedman, "5 Things High-Performing Teams Do Differently," hbr.org, October 21, 2021, https://hbr.org/2021/10/5-things-high-performing-teams-do-differently.

Code 8: Build a Relationship from the Future

1. "Michael Jordan Didn't Make Varsity—at First," *Newsweek*, October 17, 2015, https://www.newsweek.com/missing-cut-382954.

2. For a comprehensive overview of imagery theory, research, and intervention on visualization, see Daniel Gould, Nicole Damarjian, and Christy Greenleaf, "Imagery Training for Peak Performance," in J. L. Van Raalte and B. W. Brewer, eds., *Exploring Sport and Exercise Psychology*, 49–74 (Washington, DC: American Psychological Association, 2002). Also see Eugenio A. Peluso, Michael J. Ross, Jeffrey D. Gfeller, and Donna J. Lavoie, "A Comparison of Mental Strategies during Athletic Skills Performance," *Journal of Sports Science and Medicine* 4, no. 4 (December 2005): 543–549, PMID: 24501566; PMCID: PMC3899670.

3. Edna B. Foa, Elizabeth Hembree, and Barbara Rothbaum, *Prolonged Exposure Therapy for PTSD: Emotional Processing of Traumatic Experiences* (New York: Oxford University Press, 2007). Visualization, technically called "imaginal exposure" in the context of trauma-focused therapy, consists of having patients intensely visualize traumatic memories, thoughts, and emotions they have been avoiding. This type of exposure, in conjunction with *in vivo* exposure, activates fear networks in ways that allow for memory reorganization and incorporation of new, healing information. Treatments that incorporate visualization are thought to be the gold standard for treating trauma-related disorders, like PTSD.

4. D. T. Gilbert, E. C. Pinel, T. D. Wilson, S. J. Blumberg, and T. P. Wheatley, "Immune Neglect: A Source of Durability Bias in Affective Forecasting," *Journal of Personality and Social Psychology* 75, no. 3 (1998): 617–638.

5. Debra Umberson and Jennifer Karas Montez, "Social Relationships and Health: A Flashpoint for Health Policy," *Journal of Health and Social Behavior* 51, no. 1 suppl (2010): S54–S66, doi: 10.1177/0022146510383501, PMID: 20943583; PMCID: PMC3150158.

6. In basic terms, memories are the brain's ability to retain the context in which an organism experiences a specific stimuli. It's this neural capability for eletrochemical retention of past data that allows us to connect experiences and create meaning out of our lives. Eduardo Camina and Francisco Güell, "The Neuroanatomical, Neurophysiological and Psychological Basis of Memory: Current Models and Their Origins," *Frontiers in Pharmacology* 30 (June 2017): 438, doi: 10.3389/fphar.2017.00438, PMID: 28713278; PMCID: PMC5491610.

7. Research shows that emotional events are privileged differently in the brain's memory systems than non-emotional events. See, for example, Kevin S. LaBar and Roberto Cabeza, "Cognitive Neuroscience of Emotional Memory," *Nature Reviews Neuroscience* 7 (2006): 54–64.

Conclusion: Rising to Power

1. For more, see, Kerry Lotsof, "Are We Really Made of Stardust?," Natural History Museum, London, https://www.nhm.ac.uk/discover/are-we-really-made-of-stardust.html.

2. V. S. Ramachandran, *The Tell-Tale Brain: A Neuroscientist's Quest for What Makes Us Human* (New York: W. W. Norton & Co., 2011).

3. For more, see Nell Greenfieldboyce, "Is the Universe Infinite?," *Morning Edition*, NPR, December 27, 2016, https://www.npr.org/2016/12/27/507063437/is-the-universe -infinite.

INDEX

ACKNOWLEDGMENTS

One of the most amazing things about the human brain is how it transforms energy, invisible electrochemical impulses, into the relationships and work that create our lives. This book rises on the energy that many people offered to me.

Scott, thank you for—in the midst of a global pandemic—reaching out with a small invitation that morphed into a great project. Your wisdom and expertise are the steady brilliance behind a project that, in no short order, changed my life. To the rest of the talented team at Harvard Business Review Press, thank you immensely.

To my Isaiah and Clara Rose, this book was born, like you, in strange and shocking ways. Of all the ways my leadership shows up, it matters most with you. Thank you for giving your energy to the creation of this book. To Eric, thank you for helping this dream of mine take flight. Your talents and generosity are a great gift. To my parents, I'm forever grateful for what you taught me about the power of making people matter.

To Kate, who showed up so early, I thought life just naturally handed out mentors like you. Now I realize I'm one of the lucky few. You changed so much about my life, and I miss you. To my friends and colleagues, too many to name, who helped me in ways too many to list, thank you.

To the people I've had the privilege to serve, thank you. Being a part of your lives has changed mine for good.

And most of all, to God, the Master Creator, thank you for the powerful experience of life and the wild experience of emotion.

ABOUT THE AUTHOR

DR. JULIA DiGANGI is a neuropsychologist who works at the inter-section of neuroscience, psychology, and the human spirit. DiGangi's academic research has examined the brain, stress, trauma, anxiety, re-silience, and relationships. Extensively published in the scientific litera-ture, she applies her research to address stress and trauma in business, educational, parenting, marital, and military contexts. Her under-standing of stress and resilience is also informed by her work in inter-national development and humanitarian aid, where she served some of the world's most vulnerable communities. DiGangi has also worked at the White House and on multiple US presidential campaigns. She is the founder of NeuroHealth Partners, a neuropsychology-based consultancy, dedicated to helping people lead their most emotion-ally powerful lives. She serves business leaders, entrepreneurs, educa-tors, parents, and couples. She regularly keynotes conferences, teaches courses, designs curricula, leads workshops, and hosts retreats.